HOLYQUEST

March 1991

For Joe Tupak,

with gratitude,

Tony Perrino

Cover photo of
the pulpit of the Unitarian Society
of Santa Barbara
by Drew Sykes

HOLYQUEST
THE SEARCH FOR WHOLENESS

Anthony Friess Perrino

SUNFLOWER INK
Palo Colorado Canyon
Carmel, Calif. 93923

DEDICATION

This book is dedicated to
the congregation of
the Unitarian Society of Santa Barbara
and especially to Edythe Cozzolino
secretary extraordinare
who typed the manuscript.

I also wish to acknowledge
the assistance of
Robert and Babette Kinkead
and Herman Warsh.

—a. f. perrino

(paperback) 987654321

Copyright © 1988 Anthony Perrino
All rights reserved. No part of this work may be reproduced or transmitted in any form by any means, electronic or mechanical, including photocopying and or recording, or by any information storage or retrieval system, without permission in writing from the publisher.

Library of Congress Catalogue Card No. 88-063124

ISBN 0-931104-24-6

Table of Contents

INTRODUCTION by F. Forrester Church   vii

FOREWORD by Clark Dewey Wells   ix

PREFACE by a.f.p.   xi

PERSONAL PERSPECTIVES   1

What Makes Something Holy?   3
The Holiness of Humor   9
The Life Worth Living   17
The Trouble with Love   25

THEOLOGICAL THESES   33

The Function of Faith   35
The Hell There Is!   43
The Devil, You Say?   53
The Case for Mortality   61

MYTHOLOGICAL MEANINGS   69

The Meaning of the Incarnation   71
The Meaning of Israel   79
The Meaning of the Resurrection   87
The Meaning of Hero Worship   93

POLITICAL PROVOCATIONS   101

What Makes a Nation Great?   103
Freedom's Holy Light   111
The Holy War—Then and Now   119
The Dream of a World United   127

PSYCHOLOGICAL SUGGESTIONS   133

Trust Your Tears   135
The Subtle Sin of Self-Pity   141
The Subtle Sin of Sentimentality   149
Go for It!   156

ACKNOWLEDGMENTS

Permission to publish material from the following sources is hereby gratefully acknowledged:

Harper & Brothers, for a selection from "A Testament of Devotion" by Thomas R. Kelley, copyright, 1941 by Harper & Brothers.

Harper Brothers, for a selection from "He Was a Gambler Too...and Indifference" from "The Unutterable Beauty" by G. A. Studdert-Kennedy. Reprinted by permission of Harper Brothers.

Harper & Row, Publishers Inc. for a selection from Erich Fromm, "The Art of Loving", copyright 1956 by Harper & Brothers Publishers.

Henry Holt & Company, Inc. for use of four lines of "Stopping by Woods on A Snowy Evening" from THE POETRY OF ROBERT FROST edited by Edward Connery Lathem, copyright 1949 by Henry Holt and Company, Inc.

Houghton Mifflin Company for a selection from "J. B.: A Poem In Verse" by Archibald MacLeish, copyright 1956, 1957, 1958 by Archibald MacLeish. Copyright renewed 1986 by William H. MacLeish and Mary H. Grimm. Reprinted by permission of Houghton Mifflin Company.

The MacMillan Company, for a selection from "The Bomb That Fell on America" by Hermann Hagedorn, copyright 1946, by Hermann Hagedorn.

The MacMillan Company, for a selection from "The Little Gate To God (The Postern Gate)" by Walter Rauschenbusch from "Walter Rauschenbusch" by Dores Robinson Sharpe, copyright, 1942 by The MacMillan Company.

Pantheon Books, for a selection from "Knots" by R. D. Laing, copyright 1970 by R. D. Laing, published by Pantheon Books, a division of Random House, Inc.

Pantheon Books, for a selection from "Gift From The Sea" by Anne Morrow Lindbergh, copyright 1955 by Anne Morrow Lindbergh, published by Alfred A. Knopf, Inc. and Random House, Inc. Reprinted with an arrangement with Pantheon Books.

Scribners, for a selection from "Collected Poems" by Vachel Lindsay, copyright 1914 by The MacMillan Co., renewed 1942 by Elizabeth Lindsay Scribners.

The Viking Press, for a selection from "The Grapes of Wrath" by John Steinbeck, copyright, 1939 by John Steinbeck.

Introduction

Sermon collections are tricky. A good sermon is made for the ear, not the eye. What works in the context of a worship service often does not translate to the written page. Far more than an essay, or even a lecture, a sermon is a dialogue, incomplete without the unspoken response of a congregation, especially one who knows its minister well. Late last century, the great liberal preacher Phillips Brooks defined preaching as the expression of "truth through personality." The problem with most sermon collections is that, stripped of personality, the truth, however eloquently professed, fails to capture the reader's imagination. It neither engages the mind nor touches the heart.

This collection is different for one very special reason—Tony Perrino himself. His personality, and thus his truth, shines through. One doesn't read these sermons so much as hear them. Without ever obtruding himself, Tony is present: his gentle strength; his quiet fervor; his unprepossessing authority. Filled with felt thought and thought-out feeling, these sermons are sufficiently multi-dimensional to fulfill Brooks' dictum. Both heart and mind are engaged here.

In some ways Tony is a traditional preacher. He clearly states his theme, develops it in a coherent, often three-part structure, and then draws the points together in a concise summation. Yet, if the sermons are conventional in form, his style is informal and his thoughts unconventional. He writes in unforced yet poetic prose, and his sermons are distinguished by a richness of illustration, mostly in the form of the well-chosen witticism or parable. Above all, they are simple—clear and accessible, without pretention. Each of the sermons collected here makes both for fun and for profitable reading.

My sister-in-law, no easy critic, once said to me after hearing Tony preach, "I liked him, and I learned something."

I know just what she meant. One can't help but like Tony—even from his words alone his kindness and generosity of spirit shine through—but he also teaches us things, the clarity of his presentation nicely revealing the clarity of his thought.

I would describe his theology as "bread and butter Unitarian Universalist." A non-dogmatic humanist (free from the aridity of fundamentalists of the left), he is open to the deeper sources of the spirit, while drawing his inspiration from many springs. There is even a real Easter sermon here! (I wonder if he dared ask his congregation to sing "Christ the Lord is Risen Today"—if so, the morning must have been perfect.)

As a companion to Tony's fine meditation manual, this collection is a wonderful addition to any liberal religious library. True to the spirit of his entire ministry, it is a real, and very special, gift.

> F. Forrester Church
> All Souls Unitarian Church,
> New York City

Foreword

These sermons—like all printed sermons—are, in one of Tony's memorable phrases, one hundred percent half true.

The other half is knowing Tony: his glad kindness (that is Yeats'), his strength that hasn't been used tyranically since old football days, his church context—one of the healthiest and most vibrant congregations you'll ever wish to see; and his out-of-the-pulpit ministry—at hospital bedsides, (where his hand's touch and "I'm with you" mean more than a dozen droning prayers), to his patient and prophetic labors for the civic and national and international good..

What you will get is some of his largeness of heart as it comes through words: his gift for composition—the beauty of rational analysis, the vitality of specificity, the hard-won art of simplicity. (A bright preacher once returned to his former homiletics professor a book of sermons of Harry Emerson Fosdick. Putting the book down the preacher said, "Anyone could have written this." He was appropriately shaken when his mentor replied, "O yeah? Try it sometime.")

So much preaching is egotistical and banal—self-serving and perversely subjective, that many thoughtful people believe the old sermon form should be taken out behind the shed and mercifully shot.

But don't do it before you read this collection—there's not a self-congratulatory "I" or a thoughtless thought in any of Tony's sermons. The guy doesn't puff or preen—he really cares, about *you* and about the abundant life potential for us all.

> Clarke Dewey Wells,
> Interim Minister
> Unitarian Church of
> Greensboro, North Carolina

A Preface

Sermons are an intimately personal mode of communication. Whereas academic discourses may be dispassionate (someone once defined a sociologist as "standing on the brink of disaster, taking notes!") good preaching wrestles with life's deepest issues and shares an emotional as well as intellectual response to them. For that reason, sermons sometimes border on "indecent exposure," as we, ministers, reveal more about ourselves than propriety (or good judgment) would warrant.

Recognizing that risk, I am willing to be identified (if not totally exposed) by the following twenty reflections. The culling of thirty years of preaching, they accurately reveal what, I think, are the major concerns of human existence. More pointedly, perhaps, they examine the facets of what I regard as life's primary objective: that of achieving a sense of wholeness.

So, dear reader, I invite you to consider these promptings of heart and mind, with the understanding that they simply represent the honest explorations of a fellow seeker after truth and meaning.

a. f. perrino
August 1988

HOLYQUEST
THE SEARCH FOR WHOLENESS

I

PERSONAL PERSPECTIVES

What Makes Something Holy?

In The Grapes of Wrath" by John Steinbeck, Casey, the illiterate preacher, tells how he discovered the meaning of the word "Holy":

I ain't sayin' I'm like Jesus. But I got tired like him, an' I got mixed up like Him, an' I went into the wilderness like Him, (without no campin' stuff). Nighttime I'd lay on my back an' look up: midday I'd look out from a hill at the rollin' dry country; evenin' I'd foller the sun down. Sometimes I'd pray like I always done. On'y I couldn't figure what I was prayin' to or for. There was the hills, an' there was me, an' we wasn't separate no more. We was one thing. An' that one thing was holy...An' I got thinkin', on'y it wasn't thinkin' it was deeper down than thinkin'. I got thinkin' how we was holy when he was one thing, an' mankin' was holy when it was one thing.

I   THE ORIGINS OF HOLINESS

Centuries ago, primitive people regarded as "holy" any experience of mysterious power which seemed benevolent. Malevolent forces, equally beyond their understanding, were similarly attributed demonic supernaturalism but not holiness. They were feared but not revered. Reverence was reserved for the kindly mysteries of life.

Thus, the American Indians regarded the fertile earth as holy, the gently falling rain as a divine blessing, the rising sun as "the smile of the Great Spirit." In other cultures: the Hindus came to regard the river Ganges as holy water capable of cleansing and renewing their spirits; the ancient

Persians revered the sacredness of fire; and the Hebrew people, noting the mysterious life-giving power of blood, placed it upon their altars as a gesture of worship: acknowledging its vital, and therefore holy, significance.

Later, any inexplicably inspiring experience (like Moses' encounter with "the burning bush") came to be regarded as "a holy event"; the place where it happened, "holy ground"; the time of its occurrence, "a holy day"; the written account of it, "holy scripture."

And when religion became more formally organized, shrines were built to commemorate the holy places, solemn festivals were designed to observe the holy days, rituals were devised to re-create the holy experience and, of course, a hierarchy of priests was erected to protect and preserve the holy truth revealed, as human beings sought to order their experience of the awesome mysteries of life.

II THE DECLINE AND FALL OF THE SACRED SENSE

With the advent of science, however, much that had been previously regarded as mysterious (and therefore holy) became subject to natural explanation. A rainbow, for example, was no longer seen as a divine omen but recognized to be a refraction of the sun's rays through a wet sky. Similarly, other so-called miracles became understood and thereby de-mystified.

And so the modern world became, in the words of one writer, "de-sacralized": the holy days became holidays: filled with revelry but little reverence; the Holy Shrines became historical curiosities, for some, and therefore money-making enterprises for others. (When, e.g. in 1960, I visited Jerusalem and the Church of the Holy Sepulchre, which marks the location of Jesus' tomb, I was greeted with a coin box on its altar, apparently for visitors to express their reverential gratitude at being in such a holy place.)

The final stage in the de-sacralization process was left to those who continued to profess belief in traditionally holy things: the supposedly devout who have reduced the Holy Bible to an answer book (reciting chapter and verse numbers like a football quarterback calling plays). They turned The Holy Sabbath, (i.e. consecrated time) into an occasion for escaping from the world and its woes exhibiting what one writer desribed as a "Coca Cola concept of religion": which wants an effervescent, sparkling sermon, attractively bottled in pseudo-psychological terminology, with few spiritual hiccups and no unpleasant aftertaste: every Sunday morning the "pause that refreshes"! But the same religiosity harbors a conception of Deity which has degenerated from an awe-inspiring reality, before whom their ancestors stood in speechless reverence, to a manipulable, cosmic errand boy whose services are hucksterd like aspirin! "Business shaky? Make God your partner and watch the profits zoom!"

It is no wonder that thoughtful people have tended to abandon such a sense of the holy. (As one person put it, "Religion is so anemic these days, it's hardly worth being an atheist, anymore.") Unitarian Universalists, of course, are especially skeptical of such superficial piety: a fact which is reflected in the story about a "firebug" who began setting religious institutions ablaze. When he burned the Catholic Church, the priest came running out with "the sacred chalice"; when he set fire to the Jewish Temple, the Rabbi came running out with "the sacred Torah"; and, when he put the torch to the Unitarian Church, the minister came running out with the coffee urn!

That does seem to represent where we are regarding "a sense of the holy." As Kurt Vonnegut confessed recently, while dedicating a college library, "I probably ought to say something holy, but I am a Unitarian and we know almost nothing about holy things!"

That's all too, sadly, true. And I am here this morning to say that we are impoverished by that fact! Indeed, the tragic irony of modern religion is *not* that the Holy is a fiction, no longer capable of any meaning, but that we seem to be running away from it as fast as we can! Not that we have lost "God", but that we are in danger of losing our deeper selves and our sense of the potential holiness of life!

I am willing to acknowledge my own susceptibility to such secularization. Like many of you, I've been so committed to a rational approach to religion and a rejection of primitive superstitions that I've neglected to cultivate a modern and meaningful sense of the holy. But as someone once wrote, "Doctors' mistakes land in the cemetery, lawyers' mistakes wind up in jail, and minister's mistakes end up in hell!" Well, lest we all find ourselves in a hell of arid intellectualism, I would launch an effort to develop a sense of "the holy" in our corporate worship. (Don't get anxious about that statement; I'm not advocating a spooky solemnity that conjures up supernatural spirits. What I mean by holy should be apparent soon and, I trust, meaningful even to rational Unitarian Universalists.)

III   THE BURNING ONENESS—IS HOLY

Clarke Wells once enumerated some of the things which can be regarded as holy, even among those of us who no longer harbor supernatural conceptions: "a sudden awareness of breath-taking beauty, a recognition of abiding truth, relationships of deep caring," indeed, "any deep reunion of the flesh and spirit." And the single thread that runs through all our experiences of "the holy" was expressed by Steinbeck's Casey: whatever contributes to our sense of all life being "one thing." (i.e. our realization of the interconnectedness of all life.)

Kenneth Boulding says it well in one of his "Naylor Sonnets" which closes with these lines:

> ...And yet, some Thing that moves the stars,
> And holds the cosmos in a web of law,
> Moves too... in me: a hunger, a quick thaw
> Of soul that liquifies the ancient bars,
> As I, a member of creation, sing
> The burning one-ness binding everything.

"The burning one-ness binding everything", that's the awareness I'm commending. And just as the words whole and holy have a common etymological derivation, that which heightens our awareness of the wholeness of life, the inextricable interrelatedness of all things is a holy experience.

Wherever it happens is a holy place (however humble);

whenever it happens is a holy moment; whatever occasions it becomes a holy object. And, I suppose if our coffee hour, after the service, does engender real, in-depth communion, the urn may be a suitable symbol of what we regard as holy. But let me illustrate the kind of moment I have in mind, and perhaps you'll agree that the coffee hour rarely fulfills the requirements.

The story is taken from the life of Eugene Debs, the labor organizer and much-misunderstood, modern saint, who truly identified with all human beings (my definition of saintliness). Debs once wrote: "While there is a lower class, I am in it; while there is a soul in prison, I am not free..." In his later years Debs, himself, was imprisoned for his political views, and while in the Atlanta jail, he learned of a Black man, a convicted murderer, dying in the prison hospital. The man, delirious with fever, was calling for his mother who could not come. Debs placed his hand on the man's fevered brow and spoke to him in a brotherly tone. The Black man replied, "Ah, mammy, I knew you'd come." Debs called for a rocking chair, picked up the man in his arms, and sang in his best dialect, "Swing low, sweet chariot, coming for to carry me home..." The guards sensing the holiness of the moment, stood by in respectful silence as the Black man died.

It is crucially significant that the word "religion," from Latin roots, literally means "to bind together," for that which binds life into a meaningful whole is holy! (Which is why the Jewish "High Holy Days," include these readings from the Talmud: "Love is the beginning and end of the Torah" and "Hospitality is the expression of divine worship.")

Albert Schweitzer once said that, "We experience God in the will to love." Martin Buber talked about the I-Thou relationship with another human being as the way we meet (indeed, create) divine reality. In more humanistic language, both were saying that we most meaningfully experience "the holy," the reality which has historically been termed God, when we open our hearts to other human beings in genuine caring.

IV MAKING WHOLENESS HAPPEN

Which leads me to one last observation. The word "sacrifice", again from Latin, literally means "to make sacred" (sacrum-facio) not to give up something (as is popularly thought) but to make something holy by giving to it of ourselves. Without the investment of our lives, our time, our energy, our vulnerability, nothing is, or can ever become holy and sacred. And it is precisely because the creation of the holy is so demanding of commitment—that most of us settle for a literally profane life. My purpose is to commend commitment to that Holyquest.

Upon my arrival in Santa Barbara, someone said, "May all your dreams become realities." Well, my greatest dream is that this sanctuary shall become a truly holy place where we, as a genuinely caring community, meet to deal with the deepest issues of life: standing by each other in times of tragedy, rejoicing in each other's triumphs, facing together a world which desperately needs a ministry we could render, demonstrating a profound sense of the wholeness of holiness of life.

It's not an easy undertaking. We are a diverse group (some are more diverse than others!), bound primarily by a fierce allegiance to religious liberty, and prone to occasional obstreperousness in the exercise of that freedom. But I honestly believe that there is no other venture as worthy of our commitment, no greater joy than that of using our lives for such holy purpose.

The Holiness of Humor

Long before anyone ever heard of psychosomatic medicine, the Book of Proverbs suggested that, "A merry heart doeth like a good medicine." That fact, that a sense of humor is a healthy thing, has become a commonplace assumption in our time. But just as the words "healthy," "whole" and "holy" have a common etymological origin, humor has a religious, as well as a physical and emotional significance.

Let me begin by defining humor as "the kindly contemplation of life's incongruities." The kindliness is essential. There must be not only a perception of the paradoxical aspects of life, but a tolerance of them. I am aware of the fact that some would define humor to include its use as a weapon of ridicule, but I am in agreement with Thomas Carlyle who contended that "true humor is not contempt; its essence is love."

I HUMOR AND HEALTH

At the first level, I would suggest that such, genuine humor is a healthy thing, which "doeth like a good medicine," because it relieves tension and punctures pretensions: enabling us to see our circumstances more clearly and deal with life's absurdities more creatively.

There's a story about a missionary who went to speak at a local Church. Long before he arrived there was a good deal of antagonism toward his visit because the people anticipated his asking for money and they "needed all the money they could raise for their own programs." (A familiar attitude?) At any rate, he came, gave his talk, and, just as the congregation feared, concluded by saying, "Now, brothers and sisters, we'll stand and sing a hymn while my hat is passed among you for contributions toward my work." Well, the hat passed up and down the rows of people, but before long everyone realized that no one was putting any money into it! And when it was finally returned to the missionary—empty, the tension was thick as he bowed his head for an offertory prayer. But the preacher kept his sense of humor and rose to the occasion by delivering the following prayer: "O, Lord, we give thee thanks that these good and generous people, in their dire poverty, have seen fit to gimme my hat back!"

Now, I submit that, if he would've passed the hat again, the missionary probably would have gotten some money. It is difficult to sustain hostility under the onslaught of such appropriate humor.

Humor is healthy because it relieves tension and restores perspective. That is not to say that it will solve our problems, but that it does have a remarkable capacity, figuratively speaking, to wash some of the sand out of the gears, so the machinery of our minds can function more effectively.

As Henry Ward Beecher once put it, "A person without a sense of humor is like a wagon without springs: jolted by every pebble in the road."

II   HUMOR AND WHOLENESS

A second, even more significant aspect of humor is the fact that it serves the sense of wholeness. If you can laugh at yourself in ludicrous circumstances, you are reflecting and re-enforcing your sense of transcendence, your identity apart from the event. You are saying, in effect, "What happens to me-- is not 'me'; I am greater than that which I experience; I am the experiencer; and, if what happens to me is funny, I can laugh at it without threatening my sense of wholeness and well-being, without being swallowed up by the event."

A sense of humor is thus an index of, and contributor to, emotional stability. To meet the disappointments and frustrations of life, the ironies and irrationalities we encounter, with laughter, is a high form of wisdom that does not strive to obscure or deny the incongruity, but yields to and integrates it into a sense of wholeness which transcends the event.

The perspective of humor is, therefore, possible only when we have a confidence in the larger worthwhileness of life—which enables us to regard its incongruities with kindly, rather than anxious or angry contemplation.

A person who has this capacity can even recognize the humorous aspects of an unpleasant circumstance, like the man Abraham Lincoln described as responding to the prospect of being tarred and feathered and run out of town on a rail, with the comment, "If it wasn't for the honor of the thing, I'd just as soon walk!"

Humor thus reflects wholeness of personality. Laughter is a way of establishing and preserving your selfhood apart from the vicissitudes of the world around you. This is why certain, cultural groups, notably the Jews and Blacks, have tended to produce humor: they had to if they were to survive in a hostile world with their identity, their wholeness, intact!

III   HUMOR AND HOLINESS

(Exit Laughter)

When, however, we move toward the deeper incongruities of life, humor changes as the element of feeling enters in.

Someone once said, "For those who think, life is cosmic; for those who feel, life is tragic." Which is probably why the philosopher Henri Bergson contended that "Humor and feeling are incompatible." But I don't agree with that statement. I *would* agree if he had said, "Laughter and feeling are incompatible," but the fact is that feeling produces the sublimest form of humorous conception: pathos. Such humor has an expression of protest in it, but retains its character as "kindly contemplation" because it lacks bitterness as it appeals to the better side of human nature, while pointing out our frailty and folly.

Herblock, the cartoonist, is particularly adept at this kind of humor. He once did a drawing which depicted a group of obviously well-fed people, gathered around a dining table heavily laden with a sumptuous feast. In the shadowy background were the hollow faces of starving, refugee children. The caption has a plump hostess saying to a portly preacher, "Shall we say grace?"

No angry diatribe here, just the artful revelation of incongruity. There is an element of judgment implied, but it is neither harsh nor vindictive. When such perception ceases to be kindly, the humor is lost in angry indignation, as it degenerates into "sarcasm" (which literally means "scratching with a hoe!") and the "wit" becomes, as one writer put it, "An angry man in search of a victim."

Even at the deeper levels, where feeling enters in, humor must reflect a tolerance of life's absurdities or surrender to cynicism and bitterness. But when we are confronted with the deeply tragic aspects of human experience, tolerance becomes more and more difficult, laughter less and less healthy.

There are many jokes which border on poor taste and some which have been accurately described as "morbid or sick humor," because they make light of tragic situations. Just on this side of a thin borderline, which separates healthy from sick humor, are many jokes regarding drunkenness, divorce and death. An example is the story of a man who called the Montreal police department to report that the steering wheel, gear shift, and pedals had been stolen from his car. An officer promised to send someone out, but, before he dispatched the patrol car, the same voice called again and said, this time with an audible hiccup, "Never mind officer; I got into the back seat by mistake!" Now that's not offensive, to me, although I might feel differently if someone I loved were an alcoholic. But a few years ago, when morbid jokes were so popular with teenagers, one of them told me a very sick story about some children who called on a neighbor-boy and asked if he could come out to play baseball. When the mother replied, "Why children, you know that Johnnie had his arms and legs amputated," the youngsters rejoined, "Yeah, we know; we wanted him to be second base." Now there's incongruity there, *but it's not funny!* To laugh at the tragic aspects of human experience is to scorn life and render it meaningless. There is derision in that laughter and profound despair in that derision.

This, I think is why Ecclesiastes wrote that "Sorrow is better than laughter." At least it takes seriously the deeper, tragic dilemmas of human existence. Whereas laughter, at this level, makes a mockery of life!

(Enter Holiness)

But Ecclesiastes, you must remember, was the cynic who also said, "Vanity, vanity, all is vanity and striving after the wind." He lacked a belief in the basic worthwhileness of life that would have enabled him to retain his sense of humor, even when confronted with life's tragic dimensions.

For a sense of humor, at the deepest levels of life, where laughter is driven out by feeling, evolves into what we call "faith." The same sense of wholeness which enables us to laugh at the superficial incongruities of existence, expresses itself, at this level, as a faith capable of integrating, if not resolving, the inherently tragic character of human existence.

The fact is that our very being rests upon a vast incongruity: we are creatures with creative capacities; we are temporal with awareness of the timeless; we are mortal with a longing for immortality. And either we have faith, from the standpoint of which we are able to say (in traditional phrasing), "Nothing can separate us from the love of God" (i.e. destroy our belief in the basic goodness of life), *or* we are overwhelmed by the incongruity of it all and forced to say, with Ecclesiastes that, because we are mortal creatures, "All is vanity and striving after the wind." Either we affirm some measure of faith in the goodness (or at least potential goodness) of life, in spite of its tragic dimensions, *or* we must surrender to the cynicism of Ecclesiastes.

From whence comes such faith? An elderly woman was once told by an admirer, "I wish I had your faith." To which she replied "If you had something to put it in, I'd give you some." Well, of course, that's what we all need: a container that will hold intact our conviction that life is fundamentally good: a context for our effort to *make* life meaningful and just, whole and holy.

What is it that enabled Anne Frank, in the midst of Nazi persecution, to write in her diary, "I still believe, in spite of everything, that people are really good at heart." What enabled Martin Luther King to sing, "We shall overcome.."

and believe it? What, down through the ages, has sustained the confidence and courage of people plagued with injustice, and misfortune, and the inevitability of death?

Traditionally, the context of such confidence has been belief in a benevolent deity: a fatherly God, whose nature is love and whose purposes, however inscrutable, are good.

But there are those of us who do not believe in a personal God: humanists whose faith begins and ends with the divine possibilities in human nature. Have we forfeited the basis for a faith in the worthwhileness of life? I think not.

The substance of that traditional belief in "the love of God" is, I think, available in human relationship. Indeed, that, I would suggest, is its actual source for all human beings. To say that "God is love," to someone who has never experienced human love, is like telling a blind man that grass is green. The concept is empty of meaning. But to give the experience of love to another person, is to put content into that concept: to give substance to what is otherwise a meaningless abstraction. And it is that substance which sustains us and enables us to believe in life, even in times of tragic misfortune.

Archibald MacLeish says all this very well in his poetic-play entitled "J. B.", a modern rendering of *The Book of Job*. In the drama, the hero, like his Biblical counterpart, is visited by all kinds of inexplicable misfortune: his business fails, his children are taken away, his health suffers, and his wife, who had urged him to "curse God and die," finally, in despair, leaves him.

Then, in the last scene, she returns, and he meets her on the porch of their home. Sarah replies,

> "I loved you. I couldn't help you anymore.
> You wanted justice and there was none. Only love."

Then J.B., contemplating the neutrality of the universe, comments:

> "He does not love. He (simply) is."
> "But we do," Sarah responds, "that's the wonder."

They cling to each other. Then peering at the darkness inside the door, J. B. says:

"It's too dark to see."

Sarah responds:

"Then blow on the coal of the heart, my darling."
"The coal of the heart?"—he asks.
"It's all the light—now," she replies.

They come forward into the dim room. Sarah lifts a fallen chair and continues:

Blow on the coal of the heart.
The candles in the Church are out.
The lights have gone out of the sky.
Blow on the coal of the heart
And we will see—by and by...

J. B. joins her in straightening chairs and adds,

We'll see where we are.
The wit won't burn and the wet soul smolders—
Blow on the coal of the heart...and we'll know,
we'll know...

The light increases as they work and the curtain falls.

All of which is to say that, in the last analysis, the context of our conviction that life is worth living (or may be made so—whatever tragedies it holds) is our awareness of caring relationship.

When our world comes crashing down, and we sit among the shattered ruins of yesterday's hopes and dreams and blithe assumptions, *it is love alone that can give us the strength to face another day:* the fact is that this fragile fabric we call humanity is held together by the gossamer threads of human affection.

The vast incongruity inherent in human nature can only be borne by those who have experienced the sustaining power of human love. And *that,* my friends, is the primary function of a religious institution: to create a community in which the sustenance of caring relationship is available to all who enter into its life: to mediate what, in theological language, is called "grace".

The Life Worth Living

A Vachel Lindsey poem says,

Let not young souls be smothered out before
They do quaint deeds and fully flaunt their pride.
It is the world's one crime: its babes grow dull,
Its poor are ox-like, limp, and leaden-eyed.
  Not that they starve—but starve so dreamlessly;
  Not that they sow—but that they seldom reap;
  Not that they serve—but have no gods to serve;
  Not that they die—but that they die like sheep.

The poem describes all too many people: their bodies may be warm but, as far as any meaningful existence is concerned, they're more dead than alive! And so, I want to share a very personal view of what I think it means to live, fully and meaningfully to live.

My concern is that of Jean Valjean in Victor Hugo's novel, *Les Miserables*: "It's a terrible thing to die, but even more horrible—never to live!" So, I will suggest four dimensions of aliveness and examine their inter-relationship:

I

Let me begin by reminding you that anything alive is growing: whether it is a plant or an animal, a human being or an institution, it cannot remain in a static condition. We are either alive and growing, or decaying and dying. (The phenomenon is best observed when you cut a flower from its roots and it begins to wilt.)

A less obvious fact is that growth involves tension. Muscular growth, for example, requires exercise, in which the muscle strains against a counteractive force such as is experienced when a weight lifter "curls" a barbell, or in isometric exercise—when one muscle is pitted against another. If anyone completely avoids such physical tension, he or she will never develop muscular strength, indeed, their tissues will atrophy. George Bernard Shaw once supposedly said, "Whenever I feel like exercise, I lie down until the feeling goes away." —which explains why this great writer was so physically frail. Not so, his intellect, however, which leads to that level of the phenomenon.

Mental and character growth also involve tension. John Dewey, the educator, once said, "We don't think until we strike a problem." That's true: only when we wrestle with hard questions do our mental capacities grow, and only when we deal with difficult decisions do we grow in character. The reason we talk of "growing pains" is that there is no growth, and therefore no life, without tension!

I stress this because, as someone once observed, "Life is a battle in which many fall from the exhausting effort of running away." i.e. they try to avoid the struggle, to escape the tension, and thereby forfeit life itself. It's an understandable inclination: every organism instinctively shuns that which causes pain. But what makes human existence uniquely significant is our capacity for creative response to painful adversity: our ability to fashion something of value out of the raw, rigorous realities of life.

It sounds trite, but it's true that "the joy is in the struggle." Ask any ballplayer how it feels to sit on the bench! It is our capacity for enduring the tension which produces the growth that makes for the joys of creativity and life.

Thus, I would suggest that there are two kinds of people in the world (and every time I say that I'm reminded of someone's comment: "Yes, two kinds: those who divide everyone into two kinds and those who don't".) But recognizing the dangers of such generalization, let me, for the purposes of discussion, propose that there are two categories of personality: those whose motto might be "Stop the world, I want to get off", who find life too demandingly complex and abandon the growth-producing struggle—to become what I call "comtemporary ancestors." And then there are those who know that the only constant in life is change, who see in the challenges of a changing existence opportunities for growth and meaning: who recognize that to avoid that struggle is to abandon life itself!

II

Now, having asserted that life is growth and growth involves tension, I would like to suggest two other dimensions of meaningful living, each of which is necessary, and contend that the inevitable tension which emerges between them is the fundamental tension of significant living.

The first of these dimensions is integrity: i.e. to live meaningfully is to cultivate and maintain an inner identity to which you are faithful in your outward behavior. Whenever we are not true to those inner convictions which shape our unique individuality, when, in little, daily compromises we betray the principles and values of our inner awareness, they shrivel up and die there, leaving us like "The Hollow Man" T.S. Eliot once described: empty, "shape without form", "shade without color", "gesture without motion", and the very basis for our identity as a person is gone!

The classic illustration of this phenomenon is Willie Loman in Arthur Miller's play, "Death of a Salesman". Willie had always told his sons that the most important thing in life was to be well-liked: that this was the key to success and happiness. And, when his sons stood over his grave, one of them said, "He never knew who he was." How sadly true: he had been so busy trying to be what he thought other people wanted him to be that he never discovered who he was: he never really lived at all!

Emerson once wrote that "Nothing at last is sacred but the integrity of your own mind." That's true because, without it, we can have nothing else; there's no one there to have anything else. But, as e. e. cummings once observed, "to be nobody but yourself—in a world which is doing its best, night and day, to make you everybody else—means to fight the hardest battle which any human being can fight... and never stop fighting!" —which leads us to the second essential ingredient of a significant life. The reason that maintaining our integrity is so difficult is that we must do so in the context of an equally significant need for relationship!

As the psychologist Eric Berne put it, "There is that in human beings—which hungers and thirsts for relationship as much as for food and water." Which is to say that we are social animals and fully alive only to the degree that we are responsively related to other human beings. Or, as the apostle Paul phrased it, "Without love (we are) nothing..." When I use the term "love", I feel compelled to explain that I mean much more than that mixture of sex and sentimentality which is depicted in Hollywood movies, where "I love you" really means "I need you" or "I want you!" What I am exalting is the capacity for genuine caring about other people, and the sharing of their hopes and fears, their joys and sorrows. The more of that kind of relationship we have, the more alive we are: the fuller and more meaningful our days.

This fact, too, needs to be stressed—for there are those who think it fashionable to affect cool detachment: an imperturbability which views the world around it with calm indifference. The pose was illustrated in an advertisement for a woman's coat which was labelled "Casually yours." The copy beneath the picture read, "This coat captures beautifully that air of informal unconcern." They call it sophistication. But I call it death! Anyone who can "keep cool," amid the suffering and injustice of the world around us, is not "sophisticated", he or she is numb. To be insensitive to the needs and hurts of other human beings is not to be fully alive! To live meaningfully is to be related responsively to other human beings. Sometimes such caring makes great demands upon us, but to shun those demands, is to abdicate life itself!

III

Which leads us back to the fundamental tension of a meaningful existence. To summarize my contention: the two things which matter most in life— are principles and persons, and the terrible tension which often emerges between our devotion to each of them, is the major burden of significant living.

It is my belief that the vital dilemmas of life involve a conflict between our desire for integrity on one hand and our desire for relatedness on the other. Some people try to avoid the dilemma by stressing one of these at the expense of the other: they exhibit principle without compassion or compassion without principle. But the fact is that either of these, divorced from the other, will become a vicious virtue or, at best, a shallow and superficial perspective on life.

Justice without mercy, righteousness without love are cold and uncreative. They produce the kind of people the little boy had in mind when he prayed, "O, Lord, make all the bad people good and all the good people nice." You know the kind of "good" people he was remembering. They're as straight as a gun barrel, morally, and as empty as a gun barrel, "spiritually". "Good as gold and fit for heaven, but of no earthly use whatsoever!"

By the same token, however, mercy without justice, love without righteousness, produce an ethically insensitive sentimentality which is just as useless! Compassion without principle is just as bad as principle without compassion. In politics the untempered stress upon principle leads to a conservatism which is deaf to the cries of human suffering. Whereas the untempered stress upon compassion often leads to a liberalism which is blind to the ethical realities of human behavior.

What's the answer? How do you resolve the dilemma? You don't! You live with it! Someone has suggested that we need to develop "cold heads and warm hearts." But I don't think there is an easy, slogan answer.

Most of us, who are trying to live meaningfully, find that on some occasions we must put principle first (as religious liberals tend to do on the separation of Church and State issue). On other occasions our concern for persons is overriding. And we constantly live with the dilemma of deciding: dealing with every question, every issue on its own merits. And this, I would suggest, is to experience a healthy, growth-producing tension: a kind of isometric exercise for the development of character.

As I once put it in verse:

our lives are known by the dilemmas we keep:
the scope of concerns which trouble our sleep.
while some are torn by tall contradictions,
others make war with petty distinctions.
where few are stretched by great opposing claims,
most people spend their days playing at little games.

IV

There's one last point I must make. What motivates the endeavor and sustains our effort to deal with the "tall contradictions," to endure the fundamental tension between principles and persons instead of playing little games? I would suggest that it is the presence of some purpose which commands our wholehearted commitment.

There's a story of a little boy who arrived at school one day and remembered that he was supposed to have brought his birth certificate. He exclaimed, "I forgot my excuse for being born!" Well, that's what all of us need: a reason for living and enduring the inescapable tension of life. Without some commanding purpose, our days are doomed to a narcissistic preoccupation with our inability to find happiness, and our whining about the fact that the world will not devote itself to that objective.

I will illustrate with a personal reference. When I was in college, I went out for track one spring. The coach knew that football players were of little value to the track team, but he was a good-natured guy and let us work out with them. One day he began to kid me by saying, "Perrino, it isn't that you run slowly, you just run too long in one spot before you move on to the next spot." Then he said something quite profound, "Seriously, Tony, I've been trying to figure out why you can run as fast as you do on the football field, and then, when you get into a race, you look like you're pulling a truck. I think I finally understand the difference. When you're running in a game, you're always chasing someone (I was a defensive back) but when you run in a race, you're concentrating so hard on the idea of running—that, under all that intense focus, your leg muscles tighten up and you can't run as fast. The next time you race, see if you can't forget about the idea of running. Forget yourself. Just look at the finish line and say, 'I've got to get there.' And see if your legs aren't looser and freer and you don't run faster."

Well, it worked. But that was not just sound track coaching, and long before Zen and sports were linked. He was making a profound observation on human experience: most of us fail to accomplish much of significance with our lives because we're so tied up in knots of self-centered concern. And it is only when we get caught up in some cause, some purpose so important to us that we forget ourselves in our devotion to it—and fully live. That, I think, is what Jesus meant when he said, "those who lose their lives will find Life."

I want to illustrate the thought with a story that was published in the *New York Times* many years ago. It told of a young man named Jesus-Only-Jones who grew up in Harlem. There he experienced a schoolteacher who was deeply devoted to her students. She always kept in touch with her former students after they graduated to take jobs and get married. Jones was one of those who went to war and years later came out a Master Sergeant. When he returned to the States, he wrote his favorite teacher. For two weeks there was no reply. Then a note came, apologizing for the delay and explaining that she had been hospitalized and was just returning to her work. The following day, Jones was waiting outside the classroom with a check to help defray the hospital expenses. He told the teacher that, when he got her letter, he remembered a poem she had taught her students. It closed with these familiar lines:

The woods are lovely dark and deep
but I have promises to keep
and miles to go before I sleep
and miles to go before I sleep.

That, my friends, is when life is worth living: when we have promises to keep, purposes to pursue, principles to affirm, and persons about whom we care.

The Trouble With Love

*the feathery flame of love
draws near...to awaken
the embers of a dream
of a life.*

*its warm caresses
soften the surface
of a weather-beaten hope
of a joy.*

*but closer still
it begins to sear,
and afraid—lest it burn
what fools hold dear
we run...and return
to a darkness drear.*

a.f.p.

I want to write more fully about "love". I do so with the realization once expressed by Aldous Huxley who wrote: "Of all the worn, smudged, dog-eared words in our vocabulary—love is surely the grubbiest! Bawled from a million pulpits, lasciviously crooned through hundreds of millions of loudspeakers, it has become an outrage to good taste and decent feelings: an obscenity which one hesitates to pronounce. And yet, it has to be pronounced for after all love is the last word." I think that's true. As I suggested earlier, love relationship is essential to a full and satisfying life. And though the term is much maligned by misuse, "love" is a word which has to be pronounced, for, without love, "our lives are nothing," empty of joy and value.

When I use the word, "love," I'm referring to that relationship, described by the psychologist Rollo May, in which we "affirm the value and development of another person—as much as our own" or, as Howard Thurman put it, "the sense of being cared about in a way that transcends merit or demerit, of being accepted so unconditionally that there is no need to pretend anything—anymore." Whenever that kind of relationship is known, whether between a man and woman, parent and child, or intimate friends, the experience sustains, strengthens, indeed gives life to human beings!

Poets have been rhapsodizing upon this fact for years but recently some social scientists have confirmed the contention. Pitrim Sorokin, the Harvard sociologist, concluded his study of the matter with these words: "genuine love manifests itself as a life-giving force, necessary for the physical, mental and moral health of human beings."

Another sociologist, Ashley Montagu, identified a disease which afflicted infants as being the result of an absence of physical affection. He named it "marasmus" (which from the Greek means "wasting away") because babies would, literally, shrivel up and die from the lack of love!

I would focus on two questions: Why does love, like the touch of a magic wand, give life to human existence? And if this is so, why do people tend to run away from such relationship? In short—"What's the trouble with love?"

I   THE THREE "R'S" OF LOVING

First, I would contend that love gives life because it releases us, from those things which drain our vitality and destroy our identity (like anxiety, insecurity and low self-esteem). And it releases us for the expression of that unique worth which is ours to express. Love does this because it is responsive to the potentialities of a person. Contrary to popular belief, it is not blind (as infatuation is blind) to the fault of another. It recognizes that there is some bad in the best of us. But it looks for and sees beyond that, the good that is in the worst of us. And because it nurtures and evokes that potential worth, love frees us to live more fully.

Secondly, love gives life because it relates us to other human beings, enabling us to experience wider, interpersonal relationships and thereby live more fully. There is an implied assumption here that should be made more explicit: that human beings need relationships to live fully. That is why solitary confinement is dreaded by criminals who are hardened to physical brutality. It's as though humankind were a huge picture puzzle—in which each person is incomplete and unfulfilled until interrelated to others. And the experience of being loved gives life because it enlarges our capacity for such relationship. Having been unconditionally accepted, we can be more charitably accepting of others. No longer dominated by our own needs, we can be more charitably accepting of others.

A newspaper contest once awarded a prize to this definition of love: "Love is that doorway through which we pass from solitude—to kinship with all humankind." Because such kinship is essential to being fully alive, the experience of love is life-giving.

If I were to express the third reason that love gives life, in the language of traditional theology, I would say that it reconciles us to God: it reveals the character of our Creator and thereby restores us to the divine love for which we were made. As Edna St. Vincent Millay poetically put it:

*A soul can split the sky in two and
let the face of God shine through.*

In more humanistic language, love overcomes the sense of alienation from "the ground of our being" and gives us what Erich Fromm termed a feeling of "at-one-ment" with life (an apt transliteration of the word "atonement.") Traditional theology asserts that the only thing which separates us from the love of God is our own sense of unworthiness, and, when Jesus demonstrated the unconditional character of God's caring (a love that persists in spite of our sin), that barrier was removed, enabling us to be reconciled to the divine love which awaits only our trusting belief.

The great Hebrew theologian, Martin Buber, has given us an insight which bridges the gap between traditional and humanistic ways of thinking about the matter: "Divine reality," he wrote, "exists between persons. The true meaning of love one's neighbor is not that it is a commandment from God which we are to fulfill, but that through it and in it, we meet God!" "We become whole," he adds later, "only by virtue of relation to another self." It is this concept of wholeness which is most meaningful to the humanistic religionist rather than the idea of reconciliation with a cosmic personality, whose existence seems a distant abstraction, if not a poetic fiction.

It's an ancient idea. Aristophanes once suggested that "originally both sexes were encompassed in one being... which was round...with four arms and legs...and one head with two faces opposite each other." But one day Zeus became angry and sliced each being down the middle creating two persons whose lives are dominated by a search for the other half of themselves. Thus, the romantic search is seen as a longing for wholeness and unity.

The theologian, Paul Tillich, once expressed a similar thought: "Love is the moving power of life, the drive toward the unity of the separated. Reunion presupposes separation of that which belongs together, and separation presupposes original unity." There is profound truth in these observations: there is a sense in which love consummates and completes our lives. I would not, however, limit the implication to "romantic love," but include every experience of genuine intimacy.

Whichever of these (theistic or humanistic) views, is your interpretation, the important fact is that love gives life because it fulfills our need for a sense of one-ness with a transcendent reality that exists within, if not apart from, human interaction. It overcomes our sense of separateness and estrangement and gives us a wholeness which a life without love lacks.

Well, so much for the power of love to give life. The longer that I live the more convinced I am that it is the crucial fact and deepest need of human experience. To put it poetically:

> *cacophonies will e'er abound:*
> *distracting, grating, greedy sound,*
> *but love's descant above the roar*
> *liltingly doth song restore,*
> *and once its melody is heard,*
> *in tender touch or timely word,*
> *no noise intimidates again,*
> *nor stills the lingering refrain.*

What, then, is the trouble with love? How do we explain the fact that often, when we are confronted with an opportunity to experience the love which releases, relates, reconciles and gives life to human existence, we run away from it? Why do we tend to flee the genuine intimacy which we so desperately need? We all do, even in the context of marriage. There are a number of interrelated reasons, I think; let me briefly cite three, all of which have to do with our capacity for risk.

II THE THREE RISKS OF LOVING

The first is suggested by a line from an e. e. cummings' poem, "Love's function is to fabricate unknown-ness". The simple fact is that loving someone will change your life! Letting yourself care about another human being is an irretrievable leap into the unknown, an invitation to a new and strange experience. And depending upon your capacity for such a radical revision of your existence, this can be either a glorious adventure or a terrifyingly dangerous risk. This is why many prefer the status quo. As mundanely dreary as it is, it's safe and comfortable because it's predictable. This, too, is why some have said that love borders on hate: when your dull but well ordered life is suddenly rearranged by love experience, you tend to resent the person responsible.

We run from love relationship because it involves venturing into the unknown: it requires our risking change.

Secondly, love demands openness and with it the risk of self-disclosure. We cannot really get close to another human being without taking off the armor we usually wear (it makes so much noise when you try to hug). And that armor conceals, as well as protects, us.

If our own sense of self-esteem is low, if we regard as unlovely that which is concealed behind the masks we wear, we will be reluctant to risk the self-disclosure that requires. That is why Erich Fromm wrote that "self-love is a prerequisite of loving others." When self-love is lacking, we tend to project all of our self-doubts on to the attitude of the other person and cannot believe that he or she would continue to love us—if they knew what we were really like. It is, of course, a self-fulfilling prophecy because we must be known if we are to be loved.

Furthermore, concealing our true identity, because of its imperfections, deprives the other person of the opportunity to give what love has to give. The movie "Love Story" was too schmaltzy for many, but I particularly appreciated one line: the hero, after his girl friend makes a very perceptive observation about his immature attitude toward his father, says, "If you understand me so well, how can you love me?" To which Jenny responds, "That's what it's all about, preppie." That *is* what it's all about, my friends; love doesn't mean "never having to say you are sorry," but it does require self-disclosure, and that's why we run away from it.

Thirdly, love demands a capacity for trust, a willingness to risk vulnerability: the possibility of being rejected and hurt by the other person. Again, Erich Fromm says it well: "...while one is consciously afraid of not being loved, the real though usually unconscious fear is that of loving. To love means to commit one's self—without guarantee, to give one's self completely—in the hope that our love will produce love in the other person. Love [then] is an act of faith.. and whosoever is of little faith is also of little love."

The complicating fact, however, is that many people have risked loving and been rejected and thenceforth exhibit what psychologists call "the burnt child syndrome." Perhaps it was when they were children and expressed the natural inclination to commit affection, only to be met with an unloving, parental response. It's especially difficult for someone, who has been hurt, to risk again the vulnerability of loving. But a wise man once said, "Those who trust everyone will be bitten; those who trust no one will be devoured!" (i.e. they will turn life into a jungle of distrust and devastation.) We run away from love because it requires the risk of vulnerability, but against that risk is a certainty: that life without love is empty and joyless! As the British theologian, C.S. Lewis wrote:

> *To love at all is to be vulnerable. Love anything and your heart will be wrung and possibly broken. If you want to make sure of keeping it intact, you must give your heart to no one, not*

even to an animal. Wrap it carefully round with hobbies and little luxuries; avoid all entanglement; lock it up safe in the casket of your selfishness. But in that casket, safe, dark, motionless, airless, it will change. It will not be broken it will become unbreakable, impenetrable, irredeemable.

Well, I've already launched into my closing thoughts: which would simply acknowledge the difficulties and dangers of loving, and then urge you to brave the risks for the prize is life itself:

Risk the change— for living is changing.
Risk being known; it is necessary to being loved.
Risk— even being hurt— for hurts will heal.

All of which is said much more poetically in this passage from "The Prophet" by Kahill Gibran with which I close:

When love beckons to you, follow him, Though his ways are hard and steep. And when his wings enfold you yield to him, Though the sword hidden among his pinions may wound you. And when he speaks to you believe in him, Though his voice may shatter your dreams as the north wind lays waste the garden. For as love crowns you so shall he crucify you. Even as he is for your growth so is he for your pruning. Even as he ascends to your height and caresses your tenderest branches that quiver in the sun, So shall he descend to your roots and shake them in their clinging to the earth. All these things shall love do unto you that you may know the secrets of your heart and in that knowledge become a fragment of Life's heart.

II

THEOLOGICAL THESES

The Function of Faith In Rational Religion

> ...faith (is) the basic attitude of a person, a character trait which pervades all his experience...
>
> While irrational faith is rooted in the submission to a power which is felt to be overwhelmingly strong, omniscient, and omnipotent, in the abdication of one's own power and strength, rational faith is based upon the opposite experience. We have faith in a thought because it is a result of our own observation and thinking. We have faith in the potentialities of others, of ourselves, and of mankind, because, and only to the degree to which, we have experienced the growth of our own potentialities, the reality of growth in ourselves, the strength of our own power of reason and of love. The basis of rational faith is productiveness; to live by our faith means to live productively and to have the only certainty which exists: the certainty growing from productive activity and from the experience that each one of us is the active subject of whom these activities are predicated. —Erich Fromm

Any student of linguistics and history soon recognizes that the rise and fall of cultures is usually accompanied by a change in the clarity and power of their language. Periods like the 4th century B.C. when Sophocles and Aeschylus wrote, or the Elizabethan Age of Shakespeare and The King James Bible, exhibit language which is powerful and compelling. While the same cultures, at other times, seem to lack such capacity for communication.

I report this because our culture appears to be experiencing a loss of language clarity. There is, of course, an abundance of new, technical terminology: words which are precise in their connotation. But when it comes to expressing the deeper dimensions of human experience, our language seems almost bankrupt of meaning. The monetary phrase is deliberately chosen: words are like coins, they can become worn smooth by constant and careless use, and, after awhile, it is difficult to recognize what they represent.

This seems especially true of religious terminology today. If, for example, I were to ask each of you what the word "God" means, I would probably get as many different definitions as there were responses! (It is, perhaps, laboring the analogy to suggest that the minting of a Susan B. Anthony dollar the size of a quarter is comparable to the practices of defining "God" so inadequately as to depreciate the significance of the Reality experienced. But that's another sermon which, incidentally, I will call: "Making a Molehill out of a Mountain!")

I want to talk about a different, religious term also very much in need of re-definition: the re-minting, if you will, of the word faith.

Some people use the term in a manner better defined as credulity: like the little boy who said, "Faith is believin' something that ain't so" i.e. conviction contrary to evidence! I experienced such a stance in a man who once said to me, "Yessir, I believe that the whale swallowed Jonah, and, if the Bible said that Jonah swallowed the whale, I'd believe that, too." Some people call that faith. I call it credulity: i.e belief in spite of evidence, a definition which does not commend itself to rational religion.

Others speak of faith in a way that can only be described as escapism because its function allows them to avoid social responsibility. Jules Feiffer, the cartoonist, once depicted two men lying on the ground. One of them confesses that he can't seem to get aroused by thoughts of nuclear war, racial injustice, starving people etc. He asks his companion, "Do you think I'm apathetic?" The friend replies, "Let's just call it faith." Such "faith" is, as it's been termed, "the opiate of the masses," and it does not commend itself to rational religion.

Still others speak of faith as though it were a tool for the manipulation of a cosmic errand-boy conception of God.

The definition is perennially illustrated in the person who attributes his or her success (whether on the athletic field or in the Miss America beauty contest) to "my faith in God."

With all these popular misconceptions, it is understandable that a skeptic once wrote, "Religion is so anemic these days, it's hardly worth being an atheist anymore!" But, of course, the fact that some people erroneously define faith should not lead a thoughtful person to reject the term completely. Some persons equate love with lust, but that doesn't make genuine love any less significant or less necessary to our lives.

So it is with "faith". And our task, whenever possible, is to reclaim and redeem such significant words, giving modern currency and value to terms for which we have no adequate substitutes, words which can communicate important dimensions of human experience. My purpose is to explore the meaning and function of "faith" in a rational approach to religion, accepting the suggestion of the New Testament writer, James, that faith expresses itself both as belief and behavior.

I   FAITH—AS BELIEF

Regarding faith as belief, the first thing I would say is that there is a place in rational religion for belief which goes beyond evidence. BUT, when we do hold views which go beyond demonstrable facts, our construct of belief should be a reasonable projection, rather than a contradiction, of available knowledge.

Everyone, to some extent, exercises such faith. For example, a scientist conducts experiments with certain assumptions which cannot be proved and sets out to verify those hypotheses. The alternative, of believing only what you can prove, is llustrated in the story of two scientists, riding on a train, one of whom observes, "Those sheep have just been sheared." To which his more cautious friend replies, "It seems to be so—on this side." Obviously, some degree of rational faith is neccessary to our lives. Our whole economic system, based on credit, would collapse without reasoned trust; marriages would soon sour if the partners had no faith in each other's love; democracy would not be possible without some faith in elected officials; and, of course, the ultimate issue, whether or not life is worth living, is finally resolved by faith.

Which leads to the second aspect of faith as belief; it is the mental activity which strives to fashion meaning, assembling the data of existence and endeavoring to weave pattern and purpose, to create cohesiveness and order out of the chaos.

This function of faith is to make sense out of life. Sometimes that's very difficult. For example, after World War II, many European writers seriously doubted that life was anything more than a cruel joke upon human beings. But there is that in human beings which refuses to surrender its "assurance of things hoped for...", and even as disillusioned a man as Albert Camus, the French existentialist, though intellectually concluding the absurdity of existence, labored long and hard to put meaning into it! (Sisyphus becoming his symbol of the human condition.) "It is in the revolt against absurdity," he wrote, "that we recapture the dignity of life." And that, my friends, is the challenge of rational faith: to address the incongruities of existence creatively. This is NOT a naive optimism that fails to recognize the harsh realities of existence. It is a stance which refuses to submit to despair as it strives to create meaning and wholeness. It recognizes that, whether or not there is meaning out there, we have the power to create meaning for our lives.

II   FAITH— AS BEHAVIOR

Well, I have already launched into a consideration of faith as behavior, so let me complete the transition by pointing out that there is no particular virtue in maintaining faith as belief. If it is, primarily, an attempt to put meaning into life, we would be foolish and self-destructive not to have such faith. As Albert Einstein once wrote, "Anyone who regards his own life and that of his fellow creatures as meaningless... is not merely unfortunate, he is almost unqualified to live!" The impulse toward meaning, which faith as belief represents, is such a fundamental drive in human nature that to maintain it, like gasping for air, is hardly an act of heroic achievement, but a matter of survival.

Faith as behavior, however, is where life with character begins. And again there are two things I would say about this dimension of faith.

First, it is faith as behavior which fulfills faith as belief: it is when we cling to our rationally-based convictions, in spite of consequence, that we verify their validity. It is when we have the courage to act on what we believe that the meaning we seek to fashion is achieved. Let me use a rather mundane illustration: in the automobile factories, motors are pre-tested before they are put on the assembly line. But they must be put into cars before they receive the acid test of adequacy: they must actually empower an automobile before they truly fulfill their function.

So it is with faith. Our beliefs may fit nicely together as intellectual conjecture, their power may seem adequate; but faith really begins when we take our convictions off the intellectual block and put them into the life process. Then, and then only, do we know their adequacy and their validity. All of which is another way of saying that the deeper truths of life cannot be fully apprehended intellectually. They must be lived to be known. It is only when we are true to the highest we know that we come to know the highest there is! It is when we are faithful in our behavior that we test and refine and deepen our understanding of what is true and good and meaningful. What I am talking about is commitment. Just as you cannot learn how to swim from a lecture on the subject, you've got to plunge into the struggle for meaning to discover whether or not there is any.

Which leads to the second thing I would say about faith as behavior. If faith as behavior is necessary to test and verify faith as belief, it is also paradoxically true that some, prior faith as belief is necessary to motivate faith as behavior.

In order for a person to risk the consequences of behavior based upon as yet unverified belief, there must be some motivation, some reason to believe in the worthwhileness of the venture. From whence does this initial faith come? Or, to put it another way, how does faith begin? It always begins, I think, by our taking someone else's word for it!

I realize that such a statement sounds very irrational, if not authoritarian, but I believe it's true. And that belief is based on rational consideration of empirical evidence. The only way any of us ever gets started on a worthy, and therefore risky, venture— is when our respect for another person's judgment enables us to accept their assurance that it is worth the risk. That person could be a parent, a teacher, a friend, anyone whose word is believed, at least until proven unreliable.

Let me illustrate the contention from an experience of my college days. One summer I taught a Red Cross swimming class to a group of boys. The most difficult thing I had to teach was what is called "the life-saving jump." It enables the rescuer to enter the water without allowing his head to go beneath the surface, so he can keep his eyes on the drowning victim. In order to accomplish this, the swimmer must do three things with his body as he enters the water: first, his legs must be in a scissors-kick position, to be quickly brought together; secondly, his arms must be extended and brought down against the water; thirdly, and most crucially, his chest must be out so that the large, broad surface hits the water and enables him to ride on it like the prow of a boat.

Invariably, the boys' fear of getting hit in the face by the water inclined them to draw in their chests and then, of course, they went under. It was difficult to convince them that if they did exactly what I described and kept their chests out there, they would not only avoid a face-full of water, they wouldn't even get their hair wet. But their fears were so strong that only when I was able to get them to take my word for the fact that the technique worked, were they able to perform the life-saving jump properly. The literal "leap of faith" had to be made on the say-so of another person whose judgment was accepted as reliable.

So it is with all of life's ventures. From infancy's first endeavor at walking, when a smiling parent's outstretched arms nurtured the faith necessary for the scary effort, to the regularly-repeated, terrifying leap into love relationship and the vulnerability it involves, every significant venture is a risk that requires belief in the reliability of the other person. Trust in persons is the foundation of every exploration of life's deeper dimensions. Faith-as-belief in at least one other human is the basis of growth.

Here again, however, we are confronted with a paradox.

The belief in persons, which nurtures the development of our understanding and our selfhood, is dependent upon belief in ourselves! That is why Erich Fromm wrote that "faith is basically a character trait." We can only believe in the goodness of people and the meaningfulness of life if we believe in our own goodness and the worthwhileness of our own lives. "What we are, that only can we see," Ralph Waldo Emerson once wrote, and that haunting sentence summarizes the matter. If we lack faith in ourslves, we cannot have faith in anyone or anything else!

All of which says to me, whatever else we may strive for as a religious community, our primary purpose must be that of nurturing human beings' faith in themselves. The most precious gift we have to give to each other is that of communicating confidence (which literally means with faith) the belief that the other person is of unique worth. To mediate such grace is not only to fulfill the function of faith in rational religion, it is to serve the Creative Process, the very purpose of life!

The Hell There Is!

Hell
is not a place
of endless torment:
forevered, physical pain
that satisfies the wrath
of vengeful deity.

It is awareness
of hurt inflicted
beyond undoing:
remorse born
of recognized wrong.

It is
the sense of isolation,
the awful alienation
which sears a
sensitive soul
with sorrow.

But sadder still
and finally,
there is
the hopeless hell:
a sensitivity to
no remorse,
no loneliness,
nothing.

—a.f.p.

The hell to be endured hereafter, of which theology tells, is no worse than the hell we make for ourselves in this world by habitually fashioning our characters in the wrong way. If we realize the extent to which we are mere walking bundles of habits we would give more heed to their formation. We are spinning our own fates, good or evil, and never to be undone. Every smallest stroke of virtue or of vice leaves its ever so little scar. —William James

For centuries orthodox Christianity has maintained a belief in Hell. Based on Biblical references, the conception has usually been depicted as a fiery furnace of endless, physical torment. One Baptist minister described it this way: "There is a real fire in hell— except that, though it will torture you, it will not consume. Your body will be prepared by God in such a way that you will burn forever!" (Some "God"!)

Jonathan Edwards, the early American preacher, in a famous sermon entitled "Sinners in the Hands of an Angry God," added this interesting observation: "The damned will be tormented in the presence of the glorified saints. Hereby the saints will be made more aware of how great is their salvation. Their view of the misery of the damned will double the ardor of the gratitude of the saints in heaven!" (Some saints!) Well, needless-to-say, liberal religion rejects this conception of Hell as a place of divinely decreed, eternal physical suffering.

We reject it first, and most obviously, because it is illogical in light of modern scientific knowledge.

We know that at death our bodies disintegrate. We may delay that process with lead-lined, bronze caskets, but eventually, inevitably our physical bodies return to dust. If anything survives death, therefore, it is a non-material entity which wouldn't occupy space or experience time, nor would it know the sensory pain or pleasure of a physical hell or heaven.

Now, in fairness, we must acknowledge that most of modern religion has recognized this and abandoned the idea of physical hell. A few preachers still speak literally of "fire and brimstone" (they all seem to be on the radio), but most clergy speak instead of "celestial," nonphysical bodies, thereby translating but not basically changing the concept.

Spiritualizing hell, however, does not deal with our deeper, moral objections to the idea. For example, the injustice of it is apparent. Few people are all bad, and not many of us would claim to be all good. Thus, arbitrarily to separate people into two categories and consign one group to eternal torment and the other to eternal bliss is, at best, an unreasonable action. Indeed, the characterizations of heaven and hell are contradictory: no genuinely virtuous person could enjoy the pleasures of heaven knowing that other human beings were enduring the terrible tortures of hell.

A related moral issue is the characterization of God implicit in the concept. It reflects a Deity who is vindictive, indeed sub-human, in his desire for revenge. The prescribed punishment of endless torment doesn't seem to fit the crime. And to maintain that such harsh and unjust treatment is God's will is to blaspheme the divine character, ascribing to it a less than human capacity for forgiveness, indeed, a monstrous appetite for inflicting suffering!

Thirdly, the idea is psychologically unsound. Fear of hell has never made a good person out of a bad one; the threat of punishment does not chasten but tends to harden the hearts of human beings. All you have to do to recognize that fact is remember how you feel when someone threatens you. Thus, liberal religion rejects the traditional conception of hell, either as a space-time reality or some kind of non-physical, divinely decreed, eternal torment for our sins.

If some of you are relieved, or at least comfortably complacent with that thought, let me hasten to add that this doesn't mean there isn't any hell! If life is to be finally just, there must be consequences to our acts, both good and bad.

The "Peanuts" cartoon strip, one of my favorite sources of philosophical insight, once depicted Charlie Brown walking down the street with a friend, followed by Snoopy, the dog. The other boy says, "Yessir, Charlie Brown, you reap what you sow in this world. You reap what you sow." The boys walk out of the picture, and Snoopy stops, thinks about the idea for a moment, and then says, "I kinda wish there were a little more margin for error!" Don't we all! And yet, we want life to be just. Our moral sense requires that there be some reckoning of right and wrong. And, I think, there is! As William James observed, "Every stroke of virtue or of vice leaves its ever so little scar." (That is literally true. As someone once said, "Beauty in youth is biological, but beauty in old age is created by character.")

So, all we need to do is look carefully at the consequences of sin we experience here and now to gain a vivid glimpse of "The Hell there is." (I use the word "sin"— simply to describe acts which are destructive of life.) We will look at three of those consequences, which can be seen as stages of degeneration into a state of self-inflicted damnation.

I

The first is the anguish of remorse. Whenever we experience a realization that we have done something terribly and irretrievably wrong (for example that we've hurt someone deeply and unnecessarily) the agony of our regret is hell.

Let me illustrate with the story of an alcoholic who, when drunk, often abused his family. One night his little boy became seriously ill, and when the father, completely sober and very concerned, bent over the bed to express some tenderness of affection, the boy shrank back and cried out to his mother, "Don't let him hit me, mama; don't let him hit me!" The anguish of remorse which that man must have experienced is a glimpse of "the hell there is!"

All of us, at one time or another, have similarly inflicted hurt beyond undoing. We can try to compensate or atone for what we've done, but as the poet put it:

The moving finger writes— and having writ
moves on: nor all your piety or wit
shall lure it back to cancel half a line
nor all your tears wash out a word of it.

To realize that fact, in light of all we have done— or failed to do— is to experience a dimension of the hell there is.

II

It is possible, of course, to escape this pain of remorse. To do so, however, leads to the second stage of hell which is the loneliness of alienation we visit upon ourselves as a consequence of our sin. To use a rather mundane example: if you were to slander someone in conversation and then, a few minutes later, see that person coming toward you, your natural inclination would be to avoid the encounter. The other person, not knowing what you've done, feels no sense of estrangement, but your own sense of guilt erects a psychological wall of separation.

Similarly, to avoid the pain of acknowledging wrongdoing, we tend to hate those we have hurt (thereby justifying our acts), and we tend to project upon others the evils of which we are capable, rather than experience the discomfort of admitting our capacity for them. Thus, as one writer put it, "we are kept asunder by our secret sins." We can surround ourselves with people and busy ourselves with superficial activity, but as long as we maintain the fortress mentality of unacknowledged wrong, we are walled in by our hiding place, isolated by our insulation. And that, my friends, is hell: the hell of estrangement and loneliness!

III

The third consequence of sin, the last state of self-inflicted damnation, is the deadening of sensitivity which eventually occurs. The apostle Paul wrote that "the wages of sin is death." That statement always annoyed me until I understood the pychological significance of it.

The fact is that, when we sin, we do deaden our capacity for experiencing life's values. We dull our sensitivity to truth and beauty and goodness. For example, a dishonest person is soon incapable of distinguishing truth from falsehood; someone who habitually abuses the loveliness of the world around us will soon fail to recognize even what is breathtakingly beautiful. A light-hearted illustration of this consequence, so prevalent in our culture, is the incident of the little girl who saw a rainbow for the first time and said, "What's it advertising?" So has our society become blinded to the beauties of nature by its preoccupation with utilitarian values.

Some people similarly look upon gestures of genuine goodness with almost paranoid suspicion: wondering what ulterior motives are being expressed. Their sins of selfishness having dulled the capacity for perceiving genuine altruism. Oscar Wilde once wrote that "a cynic is someone who knows the price of everything and the value of nothing." I would add that such cynicism is the direct consequence of sin. And, when people get to that state, they're dead! They've reached the last stage of hell: sensitive to no remorse, no loneliness, — nothing.

IV

Well, so much for "The Hell There Is..." in the here and now. Contrary to the whimsical song of Eliza Doolittle's father (in "My Fair Lady"), it takes more than "a little bit of luck" to escape these consequences of sin. But—several questions remain. Let me deal with two of them, briefly.

Some of you may be wondering, "All right, but what happens when we die? Is there any final, moral reckoning in a hereafter?" The only intelligent answer, of course, is that we don't know.

Many people are inclined to believe in a "hereafter" because, without it, life seems so incomplete and frequently so unjust. But we have no way of knowing what a life-after-death would be like. As I said earlier, what we do know is that it would not be a physical experience. We would not have bodies and therfore would not occupy space or experience time. Indeed, such an existence is so foreign to our experience that it is impossible even to imagine.

We must also consider the possibility that there is no life after death. For even though human beings have always yearned for immortality, contrary to the popular song "wishing will (not) make it so." There are those who recoil at such a thought, suggesting that, "if there is no immortality, all life is in vain." The best reply to that attitude is one made by Thomas Huxley in a letter to Charles Kingsley. Huxley's young son had died, and at the funeral service the minister read from the Bible, "If the dead rise not again, let us eat, drink and be merry for tomorrow we die." Commenting on those words, Huxley wrote, "I cannot tell you how inexpressibly they shocked me! What! Because I am face to face with irreparable loss, because I have given back to the source from whence it came—the cause of great happiness, am I to renounce my manhood and grovel in bestiality?" Of course not! A life of meaning and virtue is its own reward and does not depend upon the promise of immortality for its motivation.

My personal response to the possibility that there is no life after death, even if it means that existence is not finally just, is to feel more deeply the urgent significance of this life now and to want to use it more fully.

The second question invariably encountered by my psychological conception of hell is one that an orthodox minister once posed to me: "Wait a minute. If people can become so insensitive, so dead that they can't even feel remorse or loneliness, is that enough punishment? Aren't they getting away with it all?" (It reminded me of a verse by Ogden Nash which suggests that: "Remorse is a duffer because the wrong people suffer.")

All I can say (especially to those who call themselves Christians) is that, if you feel that death to the spirit is not sufficient punishment for sin, you've missed the whole point of religion. Because, if you've known "the abundant life," (which every major religion promises) you wouldn't be inclined to punish someone, any more than they've already punished themselves by rejecting it! When a person reaches the last state of damnation described by Auden's poem, where "There'd be no living left to die," if you feel the necessity of punishing them further in some hell fire hereafter, you trumpet the fact that something is lacking in your life!

Some reveal in subtle ways that it is an underlying envy which compels them toward such a harsh, judgmental theology. The phenomenon is reflected in a story about a woman who was telling the minister that her husband was no good. "He runs around and squanders our money in riotous living." When the clergyman commiserated with her, saying, "I sympathize with you, my dear; your husband is a miserable sinner," the lady promptly replied, "Oh, no reverend; sinner he is, but miserable he ain't; he's having the time of his life!" The vindictive desire to punish people belies an underlying psychological and spiritual emptiness that "envies the sinners their fun and the saints their joy."

Even more serious, perhaps, is the fact that this attitude of self-righteousness and hard-heartedness reveals and seals our own doom.

Herman Hagedorn has written a poem describing a man's face-to-face encounter with God. It contains these words:

> *I hastened to reassure Him, "There's nothing the matter with me. It's the other fellow that's the trouble, a hundred and thirty-five million of him." "I know all about the hundred and thirty-five million," said the Lord, and I thought He seemed a little tired as He said it, "but I don't at the moment seem able to see anyone but you."*
>
> *"Me, Lord?" I said, "How odd! I'm sure you must be mistaken. There's nothing about me that need give you even a moment's uneasiness."*
>
> *Silence rose out of the ground, straight, hard and thick as a wall. Rose like a wall between us, between the Lord and me. And my nose flat up against it, and the Lord on the other side.*
>
> *"I'm one of your troopers, Lord," I said, "I've been fighting your battles...for years and years..."*
>
> *The wall was so cold it sweated and I began to sweat, too. "You know all about it, Lord. I've run my business by the Golden Rule...Been a vestryman in the Church, a trustee of hospitals...Fought in a dozen good causes. Not an awful lot happened, but then You know how things are in this world."*
>
> *The wall got higher and thicker and colder and wetter. I had to shout to make sure that the Lord could hear me at all.*
>
> *"You can't do this to me! I'm a pillar," I cried. "I'm a cornerstone! I'm not a materialist, a scoffer. I'm one of those Christians that hold the social structure together."*

The Lord said not a word, but space began to speak. Space spoke in icicles pointed like knives. Icicles dropping on me 'til I froze and burned and bled. "I'm a good man, Lord!" I called, "I don't get the idea!"

But we "get the idea," don't we! The one thing which most assuredly rises up like a wall to separate us from the Source and Sustenance of life is our own unwillingness to acknowledge our involvement in the sins of humankind, a self-righteousness that is insensitive, unrepentant and irredeemable.

To know that at this very moment there are babies crying themselves to sleep because they are starving and to refuse to experience the pain of listening to their cries is to plunge ourselves into the hopeless hell of hard-heartedness.

I suspect that none of you has reached that point or you probably wouldn't be reading this. If you can still feel restlessness which recognizes that your life is not all that it could be, that you're not doing all that you might be doing in response to the pain and suffering in this world, recognize what a wonderfully worthwhile thing that is: that very awareness which hurts like hell—is a sign of life and a source of hope.

Just as fire cleanses and purifies while it burns, the pain of conscience contains the power to heal and make us whole: to sustain the steep ascent out of "The Hell There Is" into life as it was meant to be!

The Devil, You Say!

A few years ago a convocation of Anglican Bishops was scheduled to discuss a statement on "Exorcism." One of the clerics questioned whether, in this modern era, The Church of England still believed in the Devil. A heated debate ensued with the Dean of Windsor saying, "I'd rather believe that the Devil exists than that he does not. It explains a lot of things!" The exchange continued, then suddenly the lights began to blink and the sound system went off and on again. The clergy never determined the cause of the problem, but, apparently wishing to take no chances, they quickly tabled the matter and went on to other business.

Historically, of course, many people have believed in the Devil. Billy Graham bases his belief on the simplistic fact that "The Bible tells us so," which, of course, it does: identifying the supernatural source of evil by several, scriptural names: Beelzebub, the Adversary, and Satan, among them. This Satanic figure has been variously depicted over the centuries. In most western societies he's usually pictured as a dark and swarthy, thin-faced man with horns. But, interestingly, the Ethiopians, a dark-skinned people, portray the Devil in their art as a fair-skinned, blue-eyed blond! (Like beauty, the features of evil are "in the eyes of the beholder!")

I

Perhaps the first thing to recognize about this inclination to personify the source of evil—is that it is an understandable expression of psychological need. There's an old, rather chauvinistic story, about a minister's wife who came home one day with a very expensive dress. When her husband berated her for so straining the family budget and asked why she did it, the woman replied, "The Devil tempted me.'" "Why didn't you say, 'Get thee behind me, Satan,'" the preacher pressed. "I did," the wife explained, "but he said, 'oh, it looks nice from back here, too!'"

In addition to recognizing the psychological reasons for objectifying the cause of evil, we must also acknowledge that, historically, it was a theological step forward when human beings ceased to regard undeserved misfortune as divine punishment for some secret sin, and began to attribute it to a sinister satanic force to be resisted. Having acknowledged these things, however, I must go on to say that we, liberal religionists, tend to reject the idea of the Devil.

We would not, like some religious groups, deny the reality of evil. Indeed, to those who say that pain and suffering are illusory, I respond with the thought contained in this limerick:

*There was a faith healer from Deal
Who said, 'Although pain is not real,
When I sit— on a pin
And it punctures my skin,
I dislike— what I fancy— I feel!'*

Pain is real enough, and that which causes suffering unnecessarily, that which is wantonly destructive of life, is evil! But just as no modern, thinking person believes in the mythical figure of "Jack Frost" in order to explain the crystalline coating of ice on the early morning earth, we can and must devise better explanations for the fact of evil in our world.

II

The first and most obvious explanation is that we human beings are the cause of much of the evil that exists, much of the pain that prevails in this world. Two Sunday school children were returning home in serious discussion of their lesson. "Do you really believe there's a Devil?" one asked. The other replied, "Naw, he's like Santa Claus. It's your Dad!" Well, human beings can be as genial and generous as St. Nick or as devilish and destructive as "old Nick", unsainted.

As Shakespeare put it, "Men are sometimes masters of their fate." Which is to say that we are to some degree at least free and can choose to use our freedom for good purposes or abuse it by destructive acts. Indeed, some theologians contend that human nature is more inclined toward evil than good. Mark Twain expressed the view, through Huckleberry Finn's remark, "Bein' good is so hard, while bein' bad ain't no trouble at all."

This idea of the perverseness of human character is illustrated in the story of a little girl whose aunt came to visit and brought two identical gifts: one blue and one red. "These are for you and your brother, Skippy," the aunt explained. "Which one do you want?" The little moppet, without hesitation, fired back, "I want Skippy's!" There does seem to be an orneriness in human beings that's hard to explain. Our personal lives and the history of humankind seem to reflect a constant conflict between the creature and the creator, the demonic and the divine potentialities in human nature. But I don't think it's constructive to attribute this fact to a sinister, satanic figure. Indeed, it seems the height of irresponsibility, an expression of the demonic, rather than an explanation of it.

As William Golding suggests in his novel, "Lord of the Flies," (which, incidentally, is the literal meaning of the word "Beelzebub") the chief devil harassing humankind is our own diabolical capacity. We may "speak of the Devil," and it may satisfy a psychological need to do so, but, in Shakespeare's words, "The fault, dear Brutus, lies not in our stars [or some supernatural being] but ourselves, that we are underlings."

III

But this leaves a whole catagory of "evil" which does not originate with human beings: such things as disease, tornadoes, earthquakes etc. How do we account for what philosophers call "natural evil?" The best explanation, I think, is that we live in an unfinished, imperfect world.

Two youngsters heard in Sunday school that the first man

was made of clay. So, they thought they'd try it for themselves, and went down to the river bed to dig the clay and make a man. Before they finished, however, they were called home to lunch where they told what they had been doing. An older brother decided to have some fun with them. He slipped away early, threw their mud man into the river, and made some tracks up the bank toward the town. When the boys returned to the site of their labors, they, of course, thought that their man had come alive, so they followed the tracks hoping to see him. When they came upon a dishevelled bum sitting on a curb nursing a hangover, one of the youngsters said sadly, "If you had waited until we finished you, you wouldn't look so bad."

In one of George MacDonald's novels, a man cries out, "I don't know why God made me!" To which a friend responds, "He hasn't made you, yet. He's making you, and you don't like it." And that, I think, is what Shakespeare meant when he said, "We are underlings." In a very profound, poetic sense that is true of all of us. And not only are we imperfect and unfinished, we live in an imperfect, unfinished world, which is sometimes destructive of life.

You don't have to know anything about music to recognize, when you hear a dominant seventh chord, that it's unresolved, incomplete, and leads to something else. This same incompletion is evident in the natural world, which awaits our efforts to perfect it. And there will be "natural evil" in this world as long as it remains unfinished: there will be victims of raging storms until we learn to control the weather; there will be people dying of cancer until that dread disease is conquered, just as there were victims of polio until Jonas Salk perfected a vaccine that has almost eliminated that crippling virus.

In short, the fact that there is evil in the world which human beings did not create—does not mean that there's nothing we can do to overcome it. The Devil is not a horned monster with a harpoon tail. The Devil is doing nothing while evil rages and people suffer!

Like Dr. Frankenstein, we create our own monsters by our apathy and indifference. The poetic symbolism of "speaking of the Devil" may be superficially comforting, but a better explanation of the evil in the world is the twin-faceted fact that we live in an unfinished universe where free and imperfect human beings often manifest destructive behavior.

IV

Now we come to what theistic theologians term "the problem of evil": Why did God create this kind of world? George Orwell, in "Animal Farm", has Benjamin, the donkey, pose the problem simply: "God gave me a tail so I could swat away the flies, but I'd just as soon he'd given me no tail and no flies!"

You see, if you believe in an all-powerful creator, He or She must be ultimately responsible for all that exists, including the evil in the world. Even those who believe in "Satan" must wonder why God created him! The only alternative is a dualism which suggests two creators, one of the good and one of the evil that exists. In other words: God cannot be both all-powerful and good. As Archibald MacLeish put it in his play, "J.B.":

If God is God, He is not good
If God is good, He is not God.
Take the even, take the odd,
If God is good, He is not God. (i.e. all-powerful)

Historically, theologians have sought to resolve this issue by postulating a fatherhood concept of the Creator: contending that God, like any good father, wanted his children to grow, so he gave them freedom, and, because he also wanted their lives to have meaning, he gave them an unfinished world, with the opportunity to share in its creation. Thus, the existence of the two sources of evil are regarded as expressions of the Creator's love!

What this answer requires, of course, is a concomitant belief that the victims of evil in this world will be provided for in an afterlife that compensates them for their suffering. To put it another way: you're only going to be able to accept the fact of hunger on earth if you believe there'll be "pie in the sky when you die!" i.e. that goodness will eventually prevail, that righteousness will finally triumph. But what of those of us who no longer believe in what one theologian described as "the daddy God?" or have faith in a "heaven" where "the lame shall walk and the crooked made straight?" Is our basis for resolving the problem of evil lost? I think not.

For, whether or not they are the providence of a fatherly Creator, the two facts of life, which account for the evil we experience are still to be desired? Isn't our freedom, in spite of its abuses, and the unfinished purpose, toward which we may contribute, still the way we would want life to be?

"Freedom with tragedy," Dostoevski once wrote, "is better than compulsory happiness." The alternative is slavishness: a life devoid of dignity. By the same token, "The great joy in life, is," as George Bernard Shaw insisted, "to be used by some worthy purpose which outlasts it." i.e. without some enduringly worthy tasks to perform, life would lose its significance and its joy.

Whether or not that is as it should be, that, my friends, is the way it is, as is illustrated in one of my favorite sources of theological insight: the "Peanuts" cartoon strip. One day the acid-tongued Lucy gave Charlie Brown some sound, if overly-direct counsel. Presiding at a stand with an overhead sign reading, "Psychiatric Help - 5 cents," she engages in this dialogue with "the patient."

Charlie: "I'm in sad shape...what can you do when life seems to be passing you by?" "Follow me," says Lucy. "I want to show you something...See that horizon over there? See how big the world is? See how much room there is for everybody? Have you seen any other world?" "No," says Charlie.

Lucy: "As far as you know this is the only world there is...right?"

Charlie: "Right."

Lucy: "There are no other worlds for you to live in...right?"

Charlie: "Right."

Then Lucy: (shouting) says, "Well, live in it, then!"
And with that verbal shock treatment Charlie Brown is powered into his familiar somersault!

This advice is not as cynical as it sounds. We all live in a world that is less than ideal and experience at least some of its destructive dimensions. The crucial question for each of us is whether we respond to that reality with whimpering self-pity or a defiant determination to resist its power.

Lewis Mumford, writing about Melville's "Moby Dick" put it this way:

> *Our ultimate defense against the universe, against evil and accident and malice, is not by any ficticious resolution of these things into an absolute which justifies them...[we] must create a realm which is independent of these hostile forces and cannot be shaken by their onslaughts. The universe is inscrutable, unfathomable, malicious...so like the white whale and its elements. And art, in the broad sense of all humanizing efforts, is our answer to this condition; for it is the means by which we circumvent our own doom...and bravely meet our tragic destiny. Not a tame and gentle bliss, but disaster, heroically encountered, is our true happy ending.*

I'll simply say, "Amen" to that. Greatness of living comes not from cursing the fates or bemoaning the evil that abounds in this world nor from irresponsibly attributing it to some Satanic figure, but from recognizing that the very realities which make evil possible are the raw materials for making life worthwhile—and joyous, my friends, and joyous!

The Case For Mortality

I kept wondering how it is to be. How incredible and splendid it is. How strange it is and mournful and fine. I'll go back at the beginning if I can...the beginning I mean—is when you come out of the dream being dreamed by the universe and feel the lonely, fierce glory of being, of being out of emptiness, of being related to and part of a great source of energy, of being an entity, whole and perishable, benign and malignant...The beginning I mean—is when you know the difference between what we pretend to be and what we are: not anything but visitors of the world, borrowers of time, coming and going. Not possessors of anything but the privilege of inhabiting substance and enduring time. -William Saroyan

I dreamed I was clutching at the face of a rock but it would not hold. Gravel gave way. I grasped for a shrub, but it pulled loose, and in cold terror I fell into the abyss. Suddenly I realized that my fall was relative; there was no bottom and no end. A feeling of pleasure overcame me. I realized that what I embody, the principle of life, cannot be destroyed. It is written in the cosmic code, the order of the universe. As I continued to fall in the dark void, embraced by the vault of the heavens, I sang to the beauty of the stars and made my peace with the darkness.
                                        -Heinz R. Pagels

The man who invented the plastic rose is dead. Behold his mark, his undying flawless blossoms never close but guard his grave unending through

*the dark. He understood neither beauty nor
flowers, which catch our hearts in nets as soft as
sky and bind us with a thread of fragile hours;
flowers are beautiful because they die.*
                                   -Peter Meinke

Easter is traditionally a time for extolling the promise of immortality. In orthodox Christian circles the theme for this day is, "Christ is risen, and, because he lives, we shall live—eternally." Liberal religionists tend to express the longing in more naturalistic terms: usually celebrating the advent of spring as symbolic of the renewal that is available to all living things. But the general assumption seems to be that life is good and death is bad; and, if we could live forever, either on earth (by the miracle of modern science) or in some heavenly realm, that would be a "consummation devoutly to be wished" (to reverse the meaning of Shakespeare's original phrase.)

The popular yearning is reflected in one of Woody Allen's quips, "I don't want to achieve immortality through my work; I want to achieve it through not dying!" And so, we tend to disguise death with cosmetics and deny it with euphemisms like "the slumber room" where people who have "passed on" repose in "life-like" serenity. There's an old Jewish proverb which says, "Everyone knows that we must die, but no one believes it." Well, my contention is that our lives would be enhanced if we did believe it: that mortality is not an evil but a blessing, which benefits not only the larger community (what would we do with all the people?) but can also enhance the lives of individual human beings.

Before I make my "case for mortality," however, a few words of qualification: I do not mean to suggest that there is virtue in the premature or particular death of anyone. Neither am I unmindful of the fact that separation from a loved one is very painful for the survivors. Nor have I forgotten that the process of dying, at whatever age, can be agonizing and degrading. (I've seen too much of that to forget.)

But my subject this morning is the fact of our finitude: the fact that we are mortal, the fact that life, for human beings, has a biological built-in time limit. And I would contend that (contrary to popular opinion) this fact has value.

I realize that it may seem inappropriate, if not improper, for a relatively "young man" to praise mortality before some who are his elders. And it's possible that, because of the apparent remoteness of my own death, I don't really know what I'm talking about: that only among the very old can there be any wisdom about mortality. But I persist with the awareness that, if I am in error, time will teach me otherwise, and whether or not you agree with me, the matter is worthy of our consideration. What is "the case for mortality?"

I

First of all, it makes us take life more seriously. To know that we have only a limited time to live, that "we are borrowers of time" (as Saroyan put it) is the motivation most of us need to make our lives matter. The "numbering of our days" is what spurs us to (in Kipling's words) "fill every fleeting minute with sixty seconds worth of distance run," to live with passionate intensity, treasuring and appreciating all that life offers.

In Greek and Roman mythology, the ancient, immortal "Gods", for all their eternal youthfulness, lived a shallow and frivolous existence as spectators of the mortals, who, by comparison, had depth, aspiration, and genuine feeling in their lives. The French dramatist, Giraudoux, suggests this in a play entitled "Amphitryon." There is a scene when the god, Jupiter, takes on the disguise of Amphitryon, so that he might make love to the man's mortal and faithful wife. Later, in discussing his success and failure with another of the gods, Mercury, Jupiter said of the woman, "And then suddenly, she will use little expressions—and that widened the abyss between us." "What expressions?" asks Mercury. And he answered, "She will say, 'When I was a child', or 'When I am old' or 'Never in all my life'. This stabs me, Mercury. We gods miss something—the poignance of the transient—the intimation of mortality—that sweet sadness of grasping at something you cannot hold."

I'm suggesting that we mortals miss it, too, when we do not acknowledge the fact of our mortality. Knowing we're going to die is what gives life urgency and makes life matter.

II

Secondly and similarly, an awareness of the brevity of our days heightens our aesthetic sense. "Death," wrote a poet, "is the mother of beauty." He might have meant that only a mortal being, aware of the transience of things, is moved to make beautiful creations: objects that will last. Certainly that is a way to achieve a kind of immortality (as Rembrandt, Bach, Shakespeare and others have demonstrated.)

But I would contend that the thought applies to natural beauty as well: its special significance, unlike that of objects of art, depend paradoxically, on its impermanence! Isn't the beauty of a flower derived, at least partially, from the fact that it will soon wither? Plastic roses, no matter how perfectly made, are not as beautiful as a real flower. And does not the beauty of a glorious sunset depend upon the fact that it is only fleetingly available? If the sky were constantly ablaze with color, would we regard it as beauteous?

Perhaps the poet is saying that our appreciation of beauty depends upon our recognition of the mortality of everything? Certainly, our awareness of the significance of a relationship grows when we recognize that it (and we) will not always be. It may be too much to say that mortality is the cause of beauty, but it is not at all too much to suggest that it enhances our appreciation of the beautiful and our capacity for experiencing it fully.

III

Thirdly, what is called "nobility of character" (or self-sacrifice for the sake of others) is only meaningful in the context of our mortality. It is because we are mortal that giving our life (the only life we have) to some worthy cause has such significance. Indeed, moral courage can be defined as the willingness to risk those things attached to our very survival, in order to serve such values as truth and justice and freedom. When we rise above our preoccupation with survival, for the sake of the noble and the good, we both challenge and fulfill the fact of our mortality.

By definition, the "immortals" cannot be noble. They have nothing to risk or lose. (That realization, incidentally, is the source of one of my quarrels with orthodox Christianity. By insisting that Jesus didn't really die on the cross, they rob his sacrifice of any significance!)

Again, the ancient Greek poets recognized this. When Odysseus is offered immortal life by the nymph-goddess, Calypso, he turns down her offer even though it means the end of suffering and hardship. He rejects that island paradise because to suffer, to endure, to persist in his journey home, for the sake of his family and friends, is nobly to live, and is the clear choice of this exemplary mortal in Homer's story. Moral virtue is made meaningful by our mortality.

IV

Now, having argued my case, I am aware of the fact that some of you might counter with the questions: "If mortality were such a blessing, why do so few recognize it as such? Why do most cultures reflect a longing for life after death? How do you explain the universal yearning for immortality?" I'm tempted to quote Mark Twain who once responded to the contention that immortality is proved by the fact that millions believed in it. His comment was, "They also believed that the world was flat!" But that's hardly an adequate answer.

The heart of the issue is why do we seek immortality? "Why," as one writer impishly put it, "do people who don't know what to do with a rainy afternoon want to live forever?" Is it because we want to live longer, to see more, and do more? I don't think so. I think the longing for immortality reflects a deeper deficiency than that of temporality.

The human spirit longs for and aspires to some condition, some state of being, some goal toward which our earthly activities seem directed, but which (for most of us) cannot be fully attained during earthly life. "Our reach exceeds our grasp," and it seeks more than continuance of time; it reaches for something beyond us, something which ever seems to elude us.

Our distress with mortality is simply a derivative reflection of the conflict between a transcendent longing of the spirit and the all-too-finite capacities of the flesh. What is it that we lack and long for?

Many poets, philosophers, and religious leaders have tried to tell us. And beneath their differences in metaphor, there is, I think, a consistent statement of reality. Aristophanes, the Greek philospher, speaks of the tragedy of human love and its unfulfillable aspiration. He suggests that we spend our lives searching for the other half of our selves from whom we've been separated since Zeus cleaved our original nature in two. Socrates agrees that we long for wholeness and completeness but not from union with a unique beloved. Rather, he contends, we irresistably strive for the wholeness of understanding, a wisdom which continually eludes us. We can achieve "philosophia," the love of wisdom, but we cannot, in this life, fully possess wisdom itself. And so, we feel incomplete. Judao-Christian writings teach that we are estranged from the love of God and long to be reunited with that eternal "ground of our being." (The story of the expulsion from the garden simply dramatizing that estrangement and our need for reconciliation. Erich Fromm, the psychologist, describes the tension as being the result of our capacity for imagination and reason. We can conceive of a perfection which we cannot attain.)

The important facts about all these, and other, accounts of human aspiration are the following: Human beings long not so much for deathlessness as for wholeness, wisdom, and a sense of union with the essence of life itself. This longing cannot be fully satisfied in our earthly life (at least for most of us). Hence the attractiveness of any promise of a fulfilling afterlife. Death itself, mortality, is not the defect but a reflection of that defect, and it is a reality which can motivate us to live more fully.

Albert Camus, the existentialist philosopher, put it harshly—but accurately, I think, "If there is a sin against life, it lies less in despairing of it—than in hoping for another—and evading the implacable grandeur of the one we have"

There is a Chinese proverb which says, "Never ask for more time : You already have all the time there is!" By diverting our aim and misdirecting our energies toward a hope for immortality, we undermine our chances of living well, here and now, and for satisfying to some extent, however incompletely, the deeper yearnings of our lives.

Jesus' triumph, celebrated at Easter, has not so much to do with a bodily resurrection into immortality as it does with the fact that he lived fully and nobly, and thereby achieved "the only eternity worth having."

III

MYTHOLOGICAL MEANINGS

The Meaning Of The Incarnation

The critics of Christmas miss the point when they blame its troubles on commercialism. All human celebration involves expenses—birthday gifts, bar mitzvahs, weddings, wakes, National ceremonies, or religious. Every shrine of the heart sells souvenirs on its outskirt.

No, Christmas deceives us by calling up intense emotions, and then trying to keep them sanitary, distanced, and toy-like. Its memories and camaraderie shake us like children for lost love; yet we are told that these normal emotions should all be reduced to an inhuman serenity and lack of pain.

There is nothing in the Christmas narrative to make us turn the manger into a Disneyland scene. The Gospels tell of a young couple driven out in hiding, of a king plotting murder.

Which is why Bach wove themes of the Passion into his Advent cantatas. And Casals, in his oratorio, "The Manger", finds the baby crying and cold. These men knew that saviours are found in the underground, outlawed, conspired against, and finally murdered. The good news always comes to us delivered by prophets and martyrs. It bursts out when bodies are broken like bread, spilling the messenger's blood like wine.

Becoming human is itself a kind of high wire balance act. Becoming better human beings always involves suffering. Those are the truths of Christmas; yet they are just the ones some defenders of Christmas would have us avoid.

Why does Christmas lead so easily to despair? Because Christmas heightens our memory and yearnings, our wish to love and be loved. It stretches our human capacities, often to a breaking point. Christmas is a dark and risky business—like falling in love, or beginning an adventure; like birth, sex or death; like becoming flesh and dwelling among men. —Garry Wills

I thoroughly enjoy the Christmas season. My senses delight in the colorful decorations, the delectable things to eat, and the lovely music which graces the holiday. My spirit is also nourished by the rekindling of old friendships, the mood of goodwill that generally prevails, and the poetic beauty of the nativity myth. Having said all that, I'm aware of the fact that these observances, as delightful as they may be, tend to obscure the deeper, theological meaning of the holiday. And, if I were a Christian, I would be very concerned to remember the fact that the birth of Jesus is celebrated because of the life it began and the implications of that life for our lives.

So I propose to do what I have done with Taoism, Buddhism, and other religious traditions: to examine the crucial concepts of that faith for whatever insights they may provide us. (I must say, parenthetically, that Unitarian Universalists are often more open to the wisdom found in "foreign faiths" than they are to those of Christianity or Judaism. We seem to carry too much emotional baggage from our early and usually negative experiences with those traditions. So, I ask those of you, for whom that is true of Christianity, to try thinking of all this as an exotic religious view which comes from a distant land, one which is, therefore, worthy at least of your curiosity.)

What Christmas commemorates, for devout Christians, is the "incarnation." The word literally means "into flesh," and, if we describe a woman as "beauty incarnate," we are saying that all that is meant by the word, "beauty," is reflected in her loveliness. Similarly, if we say that someone is "incarnate goodness," we are suggesting that the full meaning of that idea is revealed in the person's life. Implicit in the concept is the notion that there is an ideal reality, of which we are perhaps only vaguely aware, that is given concrete expression in our experience of its incarnation. The poet, Walt Whitman, was suggesting this when he wrote, "Music is what is awakened in us when we are reminded by the instruments..." Whether that ideal reality exists "out there" somewhere (as is implied in the song, "Somewhere there's music...") or is merely reflecting the human heart's longing for aesthetic pattern and harmony, is irrelevant to the significance of the idea. With that background, in the context of Christmas, what does "the incarnation" mean to devout Christians?

I

First, and most obviously, it is a statement about Jesus. It asserts that in the Galilean all that is meant by the term "God" was manifest. It relates the historical experience of early Christians, that Jesus awakened in them an awareness of ideal reality, which they felt to be the Creative Spirit of all life. As the Gospel of John puts it, "The light which lighteth every man had come into the world." "The word (i.e. the Logos, or source and sustenance of life) was made flesh and dwelt among us full of grace and truth." The writer of John's gospel doesn't try to explain or justify this contention with geneologies tracing Jesus' ancestry to David or with the Virgin birth story. He merely proclaims this incarnation as a compelling, subjective experience.

The various ascriptions employed by the followers of Jesus to express their experience of his impact on their lives were more poetry than theology, at first. They called him "Savior," "Redeemer," and "the Son of the living God," because their lives were transformed by the encounter with him, and they didn't know how else to express that experience. The mystery of how this happened is never resolved, except by faith. But the testimony of the sincere Christian is that of Paul's contention that "the light which shines in our hearts hath shone in the face of Christ."

Thus, the doctrine of the incarnation is first and foremost, for Christians, a statement about Jesus: that in him the Creative Spirit of all life was revealed in its fullness. Perhaps the whole idea is more palatable as described in this poetic reflection by the philosopher, Plato:

> *The souls of people, on their way to earth-life, pass through a room full of lights; each takes a taper - often only a spark - to guide it in the dim country of this world. But some souls, by rare fortune, are detained longer, have time to grasp a handful of tapers which they weave into a torch.*
>
> *These are the torch-bearers of humanity - its poets, seers, saints, who lead and lift the race out of darkness toward the light. They are the law-givers and saviours, the light-bringers, way-showers, truth-tellers, and without them humanity would lose its way in the dark.*

II

The second dimension of the Doctrine of the incarnation is often overlooked: the fact that it is also a statement about God. It says that, if the Creative Spirit of life were personified, it would be "Christ-like." i.e. it would bear the attributes of a "suffering servant" to humanity, a love that cares so much about human beings it would sacrifice itself to save them.

This was a shattering suggestion which challenged and changed the conventional ways of thinking about God. Most people then thought (as many still think) of greatness in terms of power to coerce obedience. A king possessed such power and so God, who must be the greatest of the great, was referred to as "The King of Kings." Then came this humble carpenter to say, "Whoever would be greatest among you, let him be the servant of all. I came not to be ministered unto but to minister," words which he lived out in his relationships.

Thus, those who believe that Jesus shows us the character of God are contending, whether they realize it or not, that the Creative Spirit of life, when incarnate, is not the omnipotent, almighty Boss of the Universe, but its loving servant: the Ultimate, Infinite Spirit of self-giving. And so, the poet writes, "Hearts unfold like flow'rs before thee— opening to the sun above..." because such self-giving devotion nurtures growth and prompts a desire to "make answer to that love."

Studdert Kennedy, the British writer, reflects this feeling in a poem entitled "The Suffering God." The last two stanzas read:

Father, if He, the Christ, were Thy Revealer,
Truly the First Begotten of the Lord,
Then must THOU be a Suff'rer and a healer,
Pierced to the heart by the sorrow of the sword.

Then must it mean, not only that Thy sorrow
Smote Thee that once upon the lonely tree,
But that today, tonight, and on the morrow
Still it will come, O Gallant God, to thee.

This concept of a suffering God is both a comfort and a challenge to thoughtful Christians. It is a comfort, not in the popular sense (to soothe or remove pain), but in the more literal meaning which the Latin roots of the word suggest: cum forte i.e. with strength. To believe that, whatever your anguish or sorrow, you are never alone— that a loving Creator shares that suffering with you, is a source of strength to human beings. It does not remove the pain, but sustains our courage and capacity to cope with it.

At the same time, it is a challenge to our consciences to believe that any time, anyone, experiences hunger, sorrow, or injustice, the infinite Spirit of life suffers with them. Therefore, "Inasmuch as we minister unto the least of these..." in their need, we do it unto the divine Reality. And, as Jesus added, "if we fail to do it unto them," we fail to alleviate the suffering of the eternal spirit. (This, incidentally, is the belief of "liberation theology" which has motivated Catholic priests in Central America to become political activists. They cannot simply murmur pious platitudes while people suffer an oppression which their God shares.) The incarnation is a statement about God which proclaims the Christ-like caring of the Creator.

III

If that dimension of the doctrine is sometimes overlooked (and it often is in orthodox Christianity), the third aspect of the incarnation is almost always ignored: the fact that it is a statement about human nature also. It points to a specific example of what must be a universal principle, if Jesus' humanity is at all real: that the Creative Spirit of life itself can enter and express itself in a human being: that we can contribute to the Process of an unfolding creation, participate in the very purpose of life, and thereby become one with God.

Thus, the incarnation portrays not only the humanity of God but the potential divinity of every human being. As Robert Frost put it in a poem:

> ...*God's own descent into flesh was meant as a demonstration that the supreme merit lay in risking spirit— in substantiation.*

And down through the ages many people *have* risked and some have realized this capacity to incarnate the Creative Spirit in their lives. It's not easy. As Garry Wills suggested in the reading, the challenge "stretches our capacities, often to the breaking point." "Becoming fully human" [Wills observes, and I would add, "therefore divine"] "always involves suffering... [one of the] truths some of the defenders of Christmas would have us avoid."

And so, because it's much easier to believe in Jesus than to strive to be like him, to call him "the son of God" than to act ourselves like children of "God," to say that he is the savior rather than do what we can to save those around us from degradation and despair, most people, even those who call themselves Christians, ignore this implication of the incarnation. But the only truly meaningful way to commemorate Jesus' birth is to render an incarnation of our own: to make the Creative Spirit of life real and redemptive in our lives and the lives we touch with the vulnerability of our caring.

The idea is dramatically expressed in a story related by a Brooklyn minister. One day he was stopped on the street by a little boy who begged the man to come see his sister who was ill. The girl was 15; her mother had died; her father had abandoned the family, leaving her to care for her younger brothers and sisters. She had literally worked her fingers to the bone in providing for the others, and now she was dying of pneumonia. The girl seemed to sense her imminent death and asked the minister, "Will I go to heaven?" He replied, "Of course you will, my dear." Then she said, "How will God know I belong?" The minister paused a moment then replied, "Show him your hands."

The Meaning Of Israel

Every year, on the Sunday between the Hebrew High Holy Days (Rosh Hashanah and Yom Kippur), I like to explore some aspect of Judaism. My purpose, as is true when I examine other religious traditions, is to lift up what has significance and value, rather than focus on points of disagreement. This is not difficult with Judaism. As one historian put it:

> *It took Europe sixteen hundred years after the decline of Greece to realize that our literature, science and architecture had their roots in Grecian civilization. It may take another few hundred years to establish that the spiritual, moral, and ideological roots of Western civilization are embedded in Judaism. To put it differently—the furniture in the Western World is Grecian, but the house in which Western man dwells is Jewish.*

I think that's true and I suggest that we take a look at the foundation of that "house." To do so is to discover the framework of our value system and understand the reason that a recent Roman Catholic Pope said, "Spiritually, we are all Semites."

I

Let me begin by telling you the story of Jacob, as reported in the 32nd chapter of Genesis. Jacob, some of you will remember (those who went to some orthodox Sunday school) was the son of Isaac, who was the son of Abraham, and the three of them (who lived around 1900 B.C.E.) are regarded as the patriarchs and progenitors of the Hebrew people. One night, in a dream, Jacob finds himself wrestling with a strange figure and the struggle lasts until morning when the other man says, "Let me go, for the day is breaking." But Jacob replies, "I will not let you go—unless you bless me." And the man asks, "What is your name?" And when Jacob told him, the man said, "Your name shall no more be called Jacob—but Israel, for you have striven with God and with men and have prevailed." And Jacob named that place "Peniel" saying, "For I have seen God face to face, and yet my life is preserved."

Thus, according to tradition, in that dramatic incident Jacob's name was changed to "Y-sroel"—which literally means "He who strives with God." Jacob subsequently fathered "the tribes of Israel," which eventually became a nation state that later was conquered. The notion of "Israel," for many years thereafter, was only an idea, a dream, but a powerful unifying aspiration of a scattered people. And from those days until this day, that magnificent metaphor has permeated Jewish life, making their time on this earth a drama of Ultimate significance. Indeed, for those who feel themselves called to strive with God, that is the very purpose of life: continually to wrestle with the ultimate, to create truth and justice and meaning in this world.

In many religious systems salvation is a highly individual matter: the devout seek in personal self-discipline to disassociate themselves from the corruptness of this world and thus achieve "purity of the spirit." There is no sense of responsibility for making the world a better place in which to live, no social dimension to the religious life.

In sharp contrast is Judaism's insistence that to share in the building of a better world, where "swords shall be beaten into plowshares..." is the very reason for the existence of religion, insisting that there is no salvation (literally spiritual health) without social responsibility.

Indeed, at the heart of the Hebrew conception of history is the thought that each of us can choose to be a part of the very meaning of life! And to share in the achievement of that purpose, is to gain enduring significance for our days. We can do this as individuals, and we can do it as a group, which is what the Jewish idea of "the Covenant" is all about. The ancient Hebrews saw themselves as a Chosen People: chosen not for privilege, by a God who plays favorites but called to a high, moral destiny, in the sense that all those who are responsive to the purpose of life become chosen instruments of divine will.

And so, at The Hanukkah Service, commemorating the Hebrew struggle for freedom, Jewish congregations read from their prayer book:

I am a Jew because in all places where there are tears and suffering the Jew weeps; I am a Jew because in every age when the cry of despair is heard, the Jew hopes; I am a Jew because Israel's promise is a universal promise; I am a Jew because, for Israel, the world is not finished; human beings will complete it; human nature is not yet fully created, we are creating it ourselves....

The fact, that this "calling" has been the guiding metaphor of "the people of Israel," is reflected in these statistics compiled by a sociologist:

There are approximately four billion people on this earth, of whom less than one half of one percent are classified as Jews. Statistically, they should hardly be heard of, like the Ainu tribe, tucked away in a corner of Asia, bystanders of history. But the Jews' influence is totally out of proportion to their small numbers. No less than 12 percent of all the Nobel prizes in physics, chemistry, and medicine have gone to Jews. The Jewish contribution to the world's list of great names in religion, literature, music, finance, and philosophy is staggering. (Einstein, Freud, Spinoza ...just to name three.)

As Leo Baeck, a Jewish scholar, writes: "To be created ...and yet creator...is at the heart of Jewish religious consciousness" (i.e. it is the very meaning of the word "Israel.") And so, "If someone comes to you in need," said a Hasidic Rabbi, "do not tell that person to 'wait upon God'...Act as if there were no God—and only you to provide."

II

A second, crucially important idea, which may be inferred from previous remarks and explicitly drawn from "The meaning of Israel," is the concept of human freedom. Because the Jews emphasized the necessity of human beings sharing the moral purposes of history, they also believed that human beings must be free from the dictates of lesser authorities—that they might be ultimately responsible only to that larger Reality.

This conviction was dramatically demonstrated in the behavior of the Hebrew prophets. While in other nations, as recently as the 19th century, the ruler was regarded as divine and his word was the law, in Israel a prophet could stand before the most powerful of kings and condemn his wrongs! The monarch might hate the man and wish him out of the way, but because the Jewish community supported the idea that there is a higher law, before which even Kings must bow, the prophet's freedom was protected. And so, when Nathan stood before David, pointed his bony finger at the ruler and said "Thou art the man...," the King trembled and repented.

In more recent years, when Martin Luther King exposed the cruel injustice of racism in America, when Ralph Nader accused the big corporations of callous indifference to consumer safety, when Daniel Ellsberg revealed the deception of the people by our government regarding the war in Vietnam, these men stood in the tradition of the Hebrew prophets of old. And the whole structure of our guarantees of free speech in this land, which enabled them to condemn those wrongs, rests upon the ancient Jewish idea that individual freedom is a sacred right.

It is no accident that organizations like The American Civil Liberties Union are predominantly made up of Jews. They know from painful experience how important it is to protect freedom of expression and have always been on the forefront of that struggle. As their Passover Ritual puts it:

> *We gather year after year to retell this ancient story. For in reality it is not ancient but eternal in its message and its spirit. ...we see ourselves as*

participants in The Exodus, for we must dedicate our energies to the cause there begun. In our day we shall defend the heritage of liberty!

And they have! And that is why it is so tragically absurd that someone like Louis Farrakan is fomenting animosity between Jews and Blacks. The Jews were among the first to fight for racial justice in this land (some of them, like Schwermer and Goodman in the southern voter registration efforts, literally giving their lives to that cause)! They knew that this struggle is at the heart of the meaning of Israel.

III

There is a third implication to The meaning of Israel which merits mentioning: it suggests an evolving process, rather than a personal God. If human beings can "wrestle with God and prevail," he, or she, or it—is obviously less than omnipotent and apparently still evolving the creative process we share. Kurt Vonnegut reflected such a perspective on deity when he wrote:

> *"In the beginning, God created the earth, and he looked upon it in his cosmic loneliness. And God said, 'Let Us make living creatures out of mud, so the mud can see what We have done.' And God created every living creature that now moveth, and one—was man. Mud as man alone could speak. God leaned close when mud as man sat up, looked around, and spoke. 'What is the purpose of all this?' he asked politely.*
>
> *"Everything must have a purpose?" asked God. 'Certainly', said man. 'Then I leave it to you to think of one for all this,' said God. And He went away." (from "Genesis" in* **The Day The World Ended**.*)*

A popular, unordained Jewish theologian, Woody Allen, similarly suggested once that "if God is omnipotent (considering the state of the world), He is an underachiever!" Allen's belief seems to be that God, like all of us, is in process of becoming, and he needs our help. One of the distinctive characteristics of Jewish theology has always been a recognition that it is idolatrous to make any particular conception of God the object of worship. Being a construct of human thought, any definition of Deity is imperfect, limited, and therefore must always be subject to continual development.

And so, the Jews have been uniquely capable of rethinking traditional ideas about God in light of modern understanding. Again, it is Woody Allen to whom we are indebted for a deeper understanding of the human encounter with an evolving deity. He retells the ancient story of Abraham and Isaac, which has always been sermonized upon as a paradigm of piety and devotion, in this much more meaningful manner:

And Abraham awoke in the middle of the night and said to his only son, Isaac, "I have had a dream where the voice of the Lord sayeth that I must sacrifice my only son, so put your pants on." And Isaac trembled and said, "So, what did you say? I mean when He brought this whole thing up?" "What am I going to say?" Abraham replied, "I'm standing there at two a.m. in my underwear with the Creator of the Universe. Should I argue?" "Well, did he say why he wants me sacrificed?" Isaac asked his father. But Abraham said, "The faithful do not question. Now let's go because I have a heavy day tomorrow."

And Sarah (his wife) who heard Abraham's plan grew vexed and said, "How doth thou know it was the Lord and not, say, thy friend who loveth practical jokes?" And Abraham answered, "Because I know it was the Lord. It was a deep, resonant voice, well modulated, and nobody else in the desert can get a rumble in it like that." And Sarah said, "And thou art willing to carry out this senseless act?" But Abraham told her, "Frankly yes, for to question the Lord's word is one of the worst things a person can do, particularly with the economy in the state it's in."

And so he took Isaac to a certain place and prepared to sacrifice him but at the last minute the Lord stayed Abraham's hand and said, "How could thou doest such a thing?" And Abraham replied, "But thou said..." "Never mind what I said," the Lord Spake. "Doth thou listen to every crazy idea that comes thy way? I jokingly suggest thou sacrifice Isaac and thou immediately runs out to do it."

And Abraham fell to his knees, "Sir, I never know when you're kidding. But doth this not prove I love thee, that I was willing to donate mine only son on thy whim?" And the Lord said, "What it proves is that some men will follow any order, no matter how asinine, as long as it comes from a resonant, well-modulated voice."

In a more serious vein, Martin Buber, who is truly regarded as one of the great theologians of the past century (by Christian as well as Jewish scholars), defined the Reality which has historically been termed God and poetically projected into a supernatural realm—as an Entity which is most profoundly experienced in interpersonal relationships. He contended that God is not "up there" somewhere but down here in the "I-Thou" encounters of human beings. His specific words are these: "Divine reality exists between persons... The true meaning of loving thy neighbor is not that it is a commandment from God—which we are to fulfill, but that through it and in it—we meet God." That is another dimension of the Meaning of Israel.

IV

One last comment for those of you who might have expected me to discuss the State of Israel, (and those of you who were afraid I would). Jacob, who was originally given the name of Israel, was not a saint; indeed, he was often less than admirable in his behavior (e.g. tricking his brother out of his birthright). Like all Jewish heroes, he is depicted as a flawed, imperfect human being. (Other religionists may like to make plaster saints of their heroes but not the Hebrews. Remember the Sunday schooler's description of King David as "a good and wise King—with a slight tendency toward adultery!")

But Israel, the man, the movement, and the nation (flawed and only-too-human) is, nevertheless called upon to strive with the ultimate issues of truth and justice, and I suggest that the nation of Israel is doing exactly that. When their government launched the invasion of Lebanon, ten percent of the population of that country took to the streets in protest! Can you imagine what chaos would be created if that were to happen here? And 3000 of its soldiers refused to participate in that military venture! That, I suggest, reflects the fact that, as wrong as Israel's foreign policy has sometimes been, (from my perspective) there is no nation on the face of the earth that does more wrestling with the moral implications of its actions than "that noisy little democracy."

"We are driven by an awareness that something is asked of us," Abraham Heschel once wrote, "that we are asked to wonder, to revere, to think, and to live in a way compatible with the grandeur and moral purpose of life." So, the meaning of Israel is that human beings are called to strive with God, to wrestle with ultimate reality, and render truth, justice, and meaning on this earth. It is an idea echoed in one of our Unitarian Universalist affirmations: "My life finds significance only as I identify with the creative Process."

Thus, though the question "Is life worth living?" is thought to be a question about the cosmos, it is not! It is a question about religious perspective. No one finds life worth living. We *make* it worth living! That's the message and meaning of Judaism. As one of their ancient sages put it, "I have set before thee life and the good and death and evil. Therefore choose life that thou and thy descendents may live."

The Meaning Of The Resurrection

Deep within us all there is an amazing, inner sanctuary of the soul, a holy place, a divine center, to which we may continuously return. Eternity is at our hearts, pressing upon our time-torn lives, warming us with intimation of an astounding destiny, calling us home unto itself. Yielding to these persuasions, gladly committing ourselves to the Light Within, is the beginning of true life. It is the slumbering 'Christ', stirring to be awakened within us all.   Thomas Kelly

Easter is an awkward occasion for most Unitarians. We want to enter into the joy of the season, but because we don't believe in the bodily resurrection of Jesus, celebrating this day is a bit like crashing a birthday party for someone we don't even know! So, our Easter services frequently focus on the rites of spring and to the traditional tune of "Christ the Lord is Risen Today," we sing: "Lo, the Earth Awakes Again." One of my colleagues, Chris Raible chided the practice—by writing this parody of the song:

*Sing an Easter hymn in season, Alleluia,
Even if we have no reason, Alleluia,
At the vernal equinox, Alleluia,
Imitate the orthodox, Alleluia.*

*Dressed up in the latest fashion, Alleluia,
Sing of praise but not of passion, Alleluia,
Sing of bunnies, bees and birds, Alleluia,
Sing an old hymn with new words, Alleluia.*

Well, Easter can be a happy celebration of spring, but my purpose this morning is to fly in the face of this long-standing and hallowed tradition of our faith and speak about the resurrection story, the "risen Christ," the Jesus who somehow did triumph over the cross, and does still live in the hearts and minds of millions of people! For whatever we believe about the historicity of the bodily resurrection, there's no denying the remarkable fact that the spirit of Jesus (if not his body) has survived and endured, for nearly 2000 years, as a profoundly important reality in the history of human experience. So, I will, in frankly autobiographical fashion, examine the various manifestations of that risen Christ," which I have encountered in my life-time.

I

As a small child, reared in a Roman Catholic home, my first encounter with "the living Christ" was to stare up at a huge crucifix and be told that the man hanging here was the bleeding figure of God, who came to earth to suffer and die for my sins! I remember feeling very sad and vaguely guilty about it and resolving to be good, so he wouldn't have to suffer any more. But it was a grim struggle with a heavy burden for a little boy. In this somber, incense-clouded setting I continued to experience Jesus as "high and lifted up" in statuary and stained glass. I knew him as a distant, unapproachable deity, the solemn God of Gregorian chants whose priests and nuns seemed sternly preoccupied with my learning the catechism correctly, reciting rote-prayers properly, and confessing my sins regularly!

In short, the Christ I knew in childhood was so wrapped in ritual, creed, and moralistic code that he seemed as cold and uncaring as the marble out of which he was carved! (I must say, parenthetically, that I have since come to know Roman Catholics in whom the spirit of Jesus is more real and relevant and warmly human. But that was not my childhood experience, and that is why, in my early teens, I walked away from that first encounter of the risen Christ—without any sense of loss.)

II

In my college years I became acquainted with "the pentecostal Christ"—who was contrastingly very earthy and available, whose salvation was immediate and emotional, and whose message was simple and direct: "Believe on me and be saved!" (the corollary of which, of course, is that those who refuse to accept him as Lord and Savior will surely suffer the fires of hell.) There were no ethical implications or social obligations attached to the gospel of this fundamentalistic Jesus, only a profession of faith in his divinity and an acknowledgement of my sinful need for redemption. It struck me, even then, as too simple, embarrassingly emotional, and socially irresponsible. That Jesus seemed more like a used-car salesman, hustling salvation at bargain prices, than a worthy object of reverence and commitment. So, I quickly walked away from that encounter without any sense of loss or sorrow.

III

Then I met a Methodist minister named Henry Hitt Crane and experienced, in him, a very different "living Christ." The Galilean, as reflected in the life and preaching of Dr. Crane, was neither a lofty, distant deity nor was he a shouting evangelist, full of cliches, selling what theologians call "cheap grace."

Crane's Christ was an examplar of the ethically sensitive and compassionate life: a man who had achieved divinity by heroic, moral courage and in so doing demonstrated a fullness of life available to us all: a divinity which each of us was meant to know. The Nazarene who lived in Henry Crane was a robust human being with a hearty sense of humor and an enthusiastic love of life. And his message was that the full and abundant life can only be known by those who are responsive to the suffering of others: who "feed the hungry, clothe the naked, set at liberty the oppressed," who courageously challenge the life-destroying evils of their age.

This Jesus also had a remarkable capacity for separating the evil deed from the evil doer and, while intensely hating the wrong done, maintaining a redemptive concern for the wrong-doer. In exercising this kind of discriminating love, he wrought genuine miracles in human hearts! Thus, in Henry Crane and later while at theological school in others like

Martin Luther King, I met "the Christ of the social gospel," and my life was challenged and changed by the encounter. Indeed, it prompted my decision to become a minister.

Ten years later, when I decided to leave the ranks of the Christian ministry (having recognized that this portrayal of Jesus represents a very selective reading of the New Testament), I did so to preserve my intellectual integrity, but not without some sense of loss!

IV

Then I experienced a fourth and entirely different kind of encounter with the reality of the Risen Christ. Like so many liberal ministers, I had learned in theological school to distinguish between "The Jesus of History" and "The Christ of Faith": to separate the noble teachings of Jesus from the questionable teachings about him, and, while holding onto his ethical insights, to reject the mythology which surrounded his life.

More recently however, with the help of people like Carl Jung and Joseph Campbell, I've come to appreciate the psychology of mythology and particularly the significance of the resurrection myth. I came to understand that what is important is not what it says about Jesus and whether that is historically true, but what it says about the humanity which contrived the story and whether that reflects a deeper truth about human experience (which, is what mythology is all about.)

The profoundly valid truth of the resurrection myth is that it dramatizes the process by which human beings achieve wholeness and connectedness with the larger reality of life itself. The fact is that pathos is the common lot of humanity, and only when we recognize and accept our own pain, do we link ourselves with the larger experience of the race, do we become stronger, more aware and wholly alive. Pathos is a Greek word which, in modern usage, is invariably linked with sickness: pathology, something to be resisted and rooted out. But the original meaning of the term had to do with the universal experience of being psychologically wounded, and the ennobling of life which can issue from our embracing, rather than suppressing, the hurt.

One psychologist put it this way, "As seed-making begins with the wounding of the ovum by the sperm, soul-making begins with the wounding of the psyche" and I would add, continues only when we allow ourselves to enter into and experience the growth-producing pain. Now, I'm not suggesting the Puritan notion that you seek out suffering "for the good of your soul." There really is no need for you to do that. You have already been wounded. We all have, inadvertently or deliberately by our families, friends, lovers, teachers, and by a society that narrows our experience and stifles our spirits.

Think about it for a moment: when and how were you wounded? (probably in early childhood, perhaps later.) Do you remember how you felt at the time? And most importantly, how did you respond? What life-patterns were begun by that experience?

My contention is simply this: most of us spend our entire lives running away from the pain of that wounding (it's an understandable reaction: every organism shuns that which causes pain). But because we do so, we never experience the deepening of self-understanding, the growth toward wholeness, the kinship with each other that only comes with working through the universal experience of suffering!

And from the depths of the collective human unconscious, the cosmic drama of the resurrection myth emerged, to remind us that the heroic, fulfilled, and therefore deathless life—is achieved by surmounting some crucifixion, by living through some "dark night of the soul": that "the Risen Christ" resides in you and me, waiting to be expressed and experienced. May that awareness, in all its significance, be yours on Easter Day, and may it lead your life to new meaning and wholeness, and joy, my friends, and great joy!

The Meaning Of Hero Worship

Because every religion engages in it, I would like to examine the phenomenon of hero worship, including, of course, heroines—in that consideration. (A sociologist once described his discipline as "the study of man—embracing woman..." Such a tendency toward ascribing a secondary role to women, in that as in other realms of historical observation, simply reflects the fact that the writers were men! that history is, as someone termed it, his-story.)

I will explore the phenomenon of hero worship, first, at the personal level, secondly, as a description of religion, focusing particularly on Christianity and its exaltation of Jesus.

I

Hero worship, as personal experience, is something with which we're all familiar. I'm sure that every one of you can remember someone whom you admired to the point of idolization: someone who, at that time at least, embodied the highest ideals of humanhood for you. The first thing to note about such an experience is that it represented a coming together of two factors: your psychological need for such a figure and the availability of a person to fill that need—at that time.

The second thing I would say about such hero worship—is that it can be a healthy thing—even when the hero or heroine is limited—if and when such admiration inspires growth in the worshipper. Emerson once wrote, "Our greatest need is for someone who will make us want to be what we can be" (i.e. we all need people who will motivate us toward fulfilling our own, unique potential as persons.) Thus, even though a particular person being idolized by a young boy or girl may not be an appropriate model for an adult, the experience could be beneficial if it led that youngster toward the next stage in his or her development.

Finally, I would suggest that hero worship can be unhealthy if the psychological need of the subject is greater than the character of the person chosen to fulfill that need. This manifests itself in two ways:

Sometimes the need is so great that it fastens itself upon unworthy persons, such as when a very insecure young person admires the so-called "strength" of a cold and callous but clever person. Probably the best illustrations are those of the Manson family's idolization of that sick but charismatic personality and the tragic devotion of Jim Jones' followers: who were literally led to their deaths in Guyana!

The more common and subtle perversion of hero worship occurs when the greatness of the psychological need inclines us to project perfection upon worthy but imperfect human beings, who are, therefore, incapable of carrying that burden. Sometimes the objects themselves encourage such adulation. One of my literature professors once said that the difference between Ben Jonson and William Shakespeare was that Jonson takes you to the window of truth and then stands in front of it! More often it is the subject's need for an infallible hero which is operative. But the result is the same: instead of being an agent of growth, the hero or heroine becomes the occasion of decay and death, precisely because his or her presumed perfection stifles the growth of what is uniquely individual in us.

Hero Worship, as a personal experience, is healthy only when it inspires growth and leaves you free to move on to the next level of development. (The implication being that we should either pick persons who are themselves growing or be prepared to change heroes and heroines periodically, so that we can continue to grow.)

II

Now let us turn to an examination of hero worship as an historical phenomenon, universally experienced in every age and culture. Once again it seems to represent a coming together of a people's psychological need and a person capable of filling that need at that time.

There is a dispute regarding whether history makes heroes, or heroes and heroines make history. One observer suggested that, "There are no great human beings, only great challenges which ordinary people rise to meet." Thomas Carlyle, on the other hand, insisted that, "All history—is the history of great [persons]." There is truth in both of these contentions. "Some achieve greatness, others have greatness thrust upon them," Shakespeare wrote. And the fact is that troubled times usually demand and produce heroic leadership. But those who arise as leaders are those particularly capable of meeting the challenge and thereby impacting history. The best example is that of Martin Luther King Jr. who once said to me, "Tony, I just happened to be in the right place at the right time." Well, his modesty was commendable, but the obvious fact is that Dr. King had "the stuff of which heroes are made" or he wouldn't have been able to rise to the occasion. Whether history is the cause or effect, the clear reality is that hero worship is a common, crucial factor in the life and destiny of nations.

And, again, we must recognize that this can be a healthy thing, even when the hero or heroine is of limited stature if he or she inspires the character growth of that culture at that time. Just as is true of a young person, someone may be, if only temporarily, an appropriate heroine or hero for a nation. Whereas, at another moment in time, be incapable of fulfilling that function. The best example is that of Winston Churchill who was probably the best person to lead Britain during World War II: his dramatic eloquence inspiring great determination and courage during that nation's darkest hour. But as a peace-time Prime Minister, Churchill failed miserably and was voted out of office!

The repeated history of hero worship, as a social phenomenon, is that the exalted figures come and go as the needs of nations change, and that is usually a healthy sign of the continuing development of the culture: an index of its psychosocial growth. But the inescapable fact of history is that hero worship can be a destructive phenomenon, as demagogues rise to fill the vacuum of leaderless society.

The most obvious illustration of a nation's psychological need being greater than the available heroes was evidenced in Nazi Germany's idolization of Adolf Hitler! It's hard to believe that this demonic figure was worshipped by so many, but in 1940 a German pilot, only 20 years old, was shot down over London, and his dying words were a request for a picture of Hitler which he could gaze upon with reverence.

Again, however, the more common and subtle perversion of hero worship occurs when an admirable but all-too-human figure is ascribed superhuman perfection, and thereby corrupted by such veneration. Just as "power tends to corrupt" few people are able to resist such a temptation to tyranny. Most persons will begin to believe that they have a divinely-appointed role to play: a "Napoleonic complex" is the name given to such an affliction after one hero suffered from it!

This "deification" is sometimes visited upon people after their deaths, as is suggested by one of my favorite quotes: "The retribution which history visits upon its great figures—is to give them followers!" The followers, of course, tend to make the hero's thoughts and views a matter of sacred dogma: the final, full revelation of truth. But such rigidity of belief (I like to call it "a hardening of the categories") discourages further exploration and development, becoming an agent of decay, rather than growth. Hero worship, as a social phenomenon, is often a healthy thing, but, when the hero or heroine is deified, the result is inescapably destructive of human welfare.

III

Which leads us to an examination of religion as hero worship. Most religions are built around the lives and teachings of heroic figures: Taoism venerates the writings of the ancient Chinese sage, Lao-Tzu; Buddhism enshrines the example and wisdom of Gotama; Judaism reveres the name and reads the Torah of Moses; Islam recites the Koran and exalts its author Mohammed, as the messenger of Allah; and, of course, Christianity is based upon the teachings of, and even more significantly the teachings about—Jesus.

In every instance, however, the religious leaders themselves sought to discourage any attempt to attribute divinity to their persons, or infallibility to their words. (That again was the retribution visited upon them by their followers.) Gotama's advice to his disciples was, "Be ye lamps unto yourselves..." (Or as someone put it more recently, "If you meet the Buddha on the road, kill him!" lest your own, unique understanding of truth be stifled by the encounter.) Moses saw himself as unworthy even to be a spokesman for God and as a good Jew, would've regarded the deification of any human being as blasphemous idolatry! (Indeed, one of the Kings who had conquered Israel complained that "These Jews do not make good slaves. There's something about their stupid religion that unfits them for subjection." That something— was and is, I think, their unwillingness to ascribe divine authority to any human being, even a King!)

Jesus of Nazareth, a thoroughgoing and devout Jew, must have shared that view. He is quoted in the oldest and most historically reliable Gospel (that of Mark) responding to someone's addressing him as, "Good master," with the words, "Don't call me 'good'; only God is good." Later, when the Gospel of Matthew was written, the statement was changed to read, "Don't ask me about the good..." as the efforts by his followers to ascribe divinity to Jesus began to emerge.

I would now like to focus on the hero worship of Jesus in the Christian faith. First I would suggest that it is a classic example of the psychological need of a people being fulfilled by a person who, in the scriptural words "came in the fullness of time." Isaiah's messianic prophecy, of one who would come and deliver the people from oppression, who would "preach good news to the poor and proclaim release to the captives..." made the people more than ready for such a hero. And so, as one writer put it, "The people heard him gladly" as Jesus gave voice to their aspirations and comfort to their afflictions

The second thing I would say is that the hero worship of Jesus did have a healthy influence on his followers at that time: helping them to live more courageously and creatively because of his words and example. The simple message of his life, which went to their hearts—was essentially this:

> *The Kingdom of heaven is within you..., and it is realized not by pious religiosity but by the maintenance of your own ethical integrity and sensitivity of the spirit.*

Jesus was aware of the evil in the world, but he urged his followers not to compound it with angry violence of their own. What he said, with his life, as much as with words, was: "Hate begets hate and hurt begets hurt...and the vicious cycle is overcome only by those who have the strength to love and release into the lives of human beings the redemptive power of such creative goodwill."

Finally, just before he went to the cross, drawing upon the motivating fact of their hero worship, Jesus said to his followers: "If you love me, feed the hungry, clothe the naked, heal the sick...for inasmuch as you do it unto the least of these...you do it unto me!" And down through the centuries millions have heeded that call to minister to the needy of the world: founding hospitals and schools, feeding the poor, serving a suffering humanity in his name, and making the hero worship of Jesus a healthy thing.

But obviously, there have also been those whose own needs led to a perversion of the regard for Jesus: by replacing the profound ethical teachings of the Galilean with a set of doctrines about him, claiming for Jesus a divine identity which he never claimed for himself. To the age-old question, "What shall I do to be saved?" (which Jesus himself answered "Love God and man"), they gave a doctrinal answer: "You must believe that Jesus Christ is the Son of God." No moral demands, no ethical imperative, just accept the dogma, and you will be saved.

This wasn't simply a perversion of hero worship, it was a betrayal of the life and teachings of Jesus himself who once said, "Not they who cry, 'Lord, Lord'—but they who do the will of God..." shall know salvation. And what is the will of God? That you "love thy neighbor as thyself!" As the writer, Dorothy Sayers observed:

> *Not Herod, not Caiaphas, not Pilate, not even Judas ever contributed to fasten upon Jesus*

Christ the reproach of blandness; that final indignity was left for pious hands to inflict. To make of his story something that could neither startle, nor shock, nor excite, nor inspire a living soul is to crucify the Son of Man afresh and put him to an open shame...Let me tell you, good Christian people, an honest writer would be ashamed to treat a nursery tale as you have treated the greatest drama in history.

That is so true. I remind you that Jesus himself was no pious sentimentalist prattling about peace on earth to a world of suffering and injustice. If he would have confined himself to such Mickey Mouse morality, we never would have heard of him! Jesus was crucified not because he said "Behold, the lilies of the field, how they grow..." but because he said, "See the thieves in the temple, how they steal!" He challenged the corruptness of his day, he exposed wrong-doing for the evil that it was, and that is why he was put to death.

It is that champion of human justice whose spirit should be remembered with a renewed commitment to his ethical challenge. Such hero worship, which avoids the pitfalls of deification and strives to emulate the example of courageous caring, commends itself—even to those of us who emphasize the humanity of Jesus.

IV

POLITICAL PROVOCATIONS

What Makes A Nation Great?

When the pilgrims came to this land 450 years ago, their pastor aboard the Mayflower read these words from The Book of Genesis: "And I will make you a great nation... and you will be a great blessing to all mankind..." Every American wants to believe that this was a prophetic event: that America has become a great nation and a blessing to all humankind. But if ours is to be an honest pride and a thoughtful patriotism, rather than flag-waving chauvinism, we must measure the stature of our nation against legitimate standards of greatness. As Carl Sandburg wrote in a poem:

> It has happened before;
> Strong men put up a city and got
> a nation together.
> And paid singers to sing and women to warble;
>   We are the greatest city,
>   the greatest nation,
>   nothing like us ever was;
> And while the singers sang
> and the strong men listened
> and paid the singers well,
> there were rats and lizards who listened
> ...and the only listeners left now
> ...are...the rats...and the lizards.

So, the question is: what makes a nation truly great? I would suggest that it is not the size of the country or its wealth or its power that are crucially relevant. To describe a nation as great is to make a value judgment, which has more to do with:

—strength of character...than physical might,
—richness of culture...than material prosperity,
—greatness of spirit...than vastness of territory.

It is especially appropriate on Memorial Day that we ask ourselves, "what makes any nation worthy of the ultimate sacrifice remembered in the holiday?"

My contention is that what makes a nation great and deserving of such devotion, are the ideals for which it stands: the human values which it serves. I will focus on three of them:

A great nation is one which is intellectually free, which allows a diversity of opinion, freely expressed, to detect and correct its errors, thus enabling it to be ever-growing and ever-capable of meeting the demands of changing times. It provides its citizens with an atmosphere which fosters creativity and nurtures individual, as well as collective growth. It recognizes that freedom is as essential to the health of a nation as air to breathe.

Secondly, a great nation is one which is morally just: maintaining laws which protect the basic human rights of all citizens, from those who would exploit them for profit. It provides programs which assist people toward social and economic justice: education for the young, security for the old, and equal opportunity for all. It regards the preservation of the civil rights of its people, as its primary purpose for existence.

And finally, a great nation is one which is a socially responsible member of the world community: one which uses its power and wealth to serve the larger interests of humankind. History is strewn with wreckage of once-mighty empires (in Voltaire's words— it is "filled with the sound of wooden shoes going upstairs and the patter of silken slippers going downstairs"). And those nations which are not mindful of the interdependence of all people are not only not great, they are doomed to disaster!

Now, using these criteria for greatness, let us measure the stature of our own nation:

I

On the test of freedom our record is generally good. We have had our dark periods, when the flame of liberty flickered: when demogogues like Joe McCarthy were able to exploit the fears of the people and convince them that certain political views ought not to be allowed free expression. But such men and moods have not gained wide following, or lasted long in our national history. Thanks to the vigilance of organizations like the American Civil Liberties Union and the diligence of the Supreme Court in upholding the principles of the "Bill of Rights," dissenters have been able to express unpopular opinions freely, without fear of arrest and imprisonment.

Recent events, however, remind me that this freedom must be regularly re-asserted, if it is to survive. It wasn't long ago that criticism of our nation's intervention in the Vietnam war was designated as disloyalty by no less a public figure than the President of the United States, Lyndon Johnson. That bit of demogoguery was repudiated, of course, by mounting numbers of protest marchers and a free press which exposed the shame of Vietnam, as it did the scandal of Watergate.

But herein lies my concern about a continuation of the freedom which has made our nation great: the people (that means you and I) must ever uphold and exericise the right of the free expression, or it will be lost. To paraphrase Mark Twain who said, "Those who don't read—have no advantage over those who can't...", "Those who don't exercise their freedom of expression—have no advantage over those who are not free." And those who stifle freedom in the name of security must be told that to do so is, eventually, to lose both.

As a great American historian Henry Steele Commager wrote: "We do not need to fear ideas but the censorship of ideas. We do not need to fear criticism but the silencing of criticism. We do not need to fear resistance to political leaders but unquestioning acquiescence in whatever policies those leaders adopt." The fact is that the only way to know when the government is wrong, to correct it and keep it strong and great, is to keep it intellectually free!

II

Regarding the ideal of justice for all, our national record is less admirable. We have made some significant gains in recent years, but the history of our treatment of native Americans, of Black people, of the poor among us and of women generally, has not lived up to our rhetoric regarding human rights.

Dick Gregory once quipped, "I wouldn't mind paying my income tax if I knew the money was going to a friendly country." Black people have particualr reason to wonder about the American promise of "justice for all." And recently we have had a government in Washington which justified its "benign neglect" of the needy of our land, by contending that welfare programs only "discourage individual initiative." But they were not averse to subsidizing wealthy tobacco farmers or discouraging the initiative of the auto industry; nor were they reluctant to write blank checks for the profiteers of weaponry: the Military-Industrial Complex, whose record of waste is a national disgrace.

If we continue to pour billions of dollars into armaments each year, while our large cities rot, we'll soon have the best protected slums in the world! And no one will have to attack us, the nation will collapse from internal decay. It's not too late to turn it around, but unless our nation does and begins to devote as much energy to the securing of human rights and economic justice as it does to military might, we can no longer think of ourselves as a great nation. We will go the way of ancient Rome into decline and fall. Unless, of course, we blow up the planet first, which leads to my last point:

III

On the matter of social responsibility among the nations of the world, again we would get mixed reviews from any objective observer. America has done some genuinely magnanimous things in the way of humanitarian foreign aid over the years. But we have also been outrageously immoral on occasion, going from isolationism to interventionism without ever stopping to try genuine internationalism!

We did so, of course, (as nations do) to serve our own economic interests. When Major General Smedley Butler retired in 1935, he described this seamy side of our history with these words:

It may seem odd for me, a military man to adopt such a comparison. Truthfulness compels me to do so. I spent 33 years and 4 months in active military service as a member of our country's most agile military force— the Marine Corps. I served in all commissioned ranks from a second lieutenant to Major General. And during that period I spent most of my time being a high-class muscle man for Big Business, for Wall Street and for the bankers...

I helped make Mexico and especially Tampico safe for American oil interests in 1914. I helped make Haiti and Cuba a decent place for the National City Bank to collect revenues. I helped in the raping of half a dozen Central American republics for the benefits of Wall Street. I helped purify Nicaragua for the international banking house of Brown Brothers in 1909-12. I brought light to the Dominican Republic for American sugar interests in 1916. In China in 1927 I helped see to it that the Standard Oil went its way unmolested. During those years, I had, as the boys in the back room would say, a swell racket. I was rewarded with honors, medals and promotion. Looking back on it, I feel that I might have given Al Capone a few hints. The best he could do was to operate his racket in three city districts. I operated on three continents!

If you are inclined to write off those words as the raving of one, confused military man, I would point out that when General David Schoup, the Marine Corps Commandant, retired during the Vietnam war, he had similar things to say about that conflict: specifically, "I believe that if we would have kept our dirty, bloody, dollar-crooked fingers out of the business of these nations so full of depressed, exploited people, they would arrive at a solution to their problems."

And now, fueled by a fanatical fear of Communism, we are engaged in an arms race that threatens to destroy the whole human family. And for some strange reason it is the retired military men who seem to be most aware of the madness of it all. President Dwight D. Eisenhower said in 1959:

> *Every gun that is made, every warship launched, every rocket fired, signifies, in the final sense, a theft from those who hunger and are not fed, those who are cold and are not clothed. We pay for a single fighter plane with a half billion bushels of wheat. We pay for a single destroyer with new homes that could have housed more than eight thousand people. Is there no other way the world can live?*

There is, of course, a better way for the world to live, and if America is to lay claim to being a "great nation," it will have to lead the way toward disarmament and the creation of an interdependent world community.

During the celebration of our nation's bicentennial, Dr. Commager wrote a "Declaration of Interdependence" based on our own founding Declaration of Independence. It reads:

> *When in the course of history the threat of extinction confronts mankind, it is necessary for the people of the United States to declare their interdependence with the people of all nations and to embrace those principles and build those institutions which will enable mankind to survive and civilization to flourish. Two centuries ago our forefathers brought forth a new nation: now we must join with others to bring forth a new world order. On this historic occasion, it is proper that the American people should reaffirm those principles on which the United States of America was founded, acknowledge the new crises which confront them, accept the new obligations which history imposes upon them...*

If the President of the United States would go before the United Nations with such an attitude, he would be reflecting the responsible character of a "great nation." But the President will do that only if the people of this land rise up and demand such leadership. The astronomer, Carl Sagan, recently expressed the urgency of the matter:

> *What a waste it would be, after four billion tortuous years of evolution, if the dominant organism on earth contrived its own self-destruction. We are the first species to have devised the means. There is no issue more important than the avoidance of nuclear war. It is incredible for any thinking person not to be concerned with this issue!*

Well, so much for my assessment of the greatness of America. Let me make clear that however severe my criticism, mine is (to paraphrase Robert Frost) "a lover's quarrel with my native land." With all her faults, I see no other nation on the earth that holds more hope for humanity or lays a greater claim on my allegiance. We have a heritage of noble ideals and, I think, the capacity to live up to them.

My purpose in writing this is to fulfill an observation made by Alexis de Tocqueville, when he visited America 150 years ago and wrote:

> *I sought for the greatness of America in her commodious harbors and her ample rivers, and it was not there. I sought for the greatness of America in her rich mines and her vast world of commerce, and it was not there. I sought for the greatness of America in her democratic Congress and her matchless Constitution, and it was not there. Not until I went into the churches of America and heard her pulpits flame with righteousness did I understand the secret of her genius and power. America is great because America is good; and if America ceases to be good, America will cease to be great.*

My faith is expressed in these words by Thomas Wolfe:

> *I think the true discovery of America is before us. I think the true fulfillment of our spirits, of our people, of our mighty and immortal land, is yet to*

come. I think the true discovery of our own democracy is still before us...and that this glorious assurance is not only our living hope, but our dream to be accomplished....'

May you and I, dear reader, help to make that happen.

Freedom's Holy Light

Men are qualified for civil liberty in exact proportion to their disposition to put moral chains upon their own appetites. Society cannot exist unless a controlling power upon will and appetite be placed somewhere and the less of it there is within, the more there is without. It is ordained in the eternal constitution of things, that men of intemperate minds cannot be free; their passions forge their fetters. —Edmund Burke, 1791

De Tocqueville was not speaking rhetorically when he said, '...there is nothing more arduous than the apprenticeship of liberty.' And he might have added that the apprenticeship is unending - the unchanging requirement of a free society's survival is that each generation rediscover this truth. —John W. Gardner

*There are those who think of liberty
as a constututional claim:
granting gross licentiousness
in sacred freedom's name.
What blasphemy of truth in that;
what folly to believe it right
that papery privilege could contain
the flame of freedom's holy light.* —a.f.p.

If the word, love, is the most maligned and misused term in the English language (and I think it is), a close runner up for that dubious distinction is the word "freedom." It is a term which, as children, we learn to pronounce with reverence, and rightly so, for genuine liberty is, without doubt, a priceless possession. But how carelessly we use, and thoughtlessly abuse, the term. For some, to be free merely means to be unbuttoned! Liberty is equated with license! And "free enterprise" is often a euphemism for the right to exploit others, without governmental interference!

In the realm of international politics, people talk of "the free world" and really mean those nations which are aligned with our foreign policy: a designation which has historically included such unfree dictatorships as that of Spain, Portugal, South Vietnam, Iran, the Philippines and Somozan Nicaragua.

There are many facets to the concept of freedom: psychological, philosophical, even religious. I would like to examine its political significance, in light of our national heritage. I do so in the context of a statement made by Jean Jaures, the French political philosopher, who once wrote, "Take from the altars of the past—the fire—not the ashes!" What a great insight! It's so obvious and yet so neglected a truth, that we must take from the altars of our nation's past—the living fire of freedom, rather than the ashen residue of its flame.

I

The first thing we must do, if we would preserve that fire, is to learn to distinguish it from the ashes! If that seems a gratuitous thing to say, consider these events: Several years ago, when U.S. troops were sent to Cyprus to help the British put down a rebellion there, some of the soldiers decided to celebrate the Fourth of July with fireworks. Villagers, hearing the noise, came running out of their homes to see what was causing the commotion. An army sergeant explained that they were commemorating America's Independence Day. One of the townspeople asked with a sly smile, "Independence from whom?" The sergeant sheepishly replied, "Oh, well, that was a long time ago." More recently in Madison, Wisconsin, a newspaperman stood on a street corner and tried to get people to sign an unidentified copy of The Declaration of Independence. Some said it sounded "too radical," others branded it "subversive" and "un-American," and not one of the 67 people who were invited to affix their names to this basic document of our democracy—would do so! And finally, not long ago, a college professor submitted a questionnaire to his students; it was designed to determine whether they would uphold the propositions put forth in the Bill of Rights of our Constitution. The results were disturbing: "More than seven out of ten students... would deny an accused person the right to confront his accuser. Four out of ten believed that there are groups to whom the rights of peaceful assembly should be denied! And more than 40 percent would deny some individuals the right to public trial and due process of law..."

To paraphrase an old gag which says that "all men are equal but some are equaller than others," there are many people in our land who believe that some of us should be freer than others. But the fact, that they would deny freedom to those who disagree with them, reveals that they don't really believe in freedom at all! Freedom cannot be selectively dispensed; either we have freedom for every citizen, or we have freedom for none. Abraham Lincoln stated the matter memorably, "Those who will not grant freedom to others, have no right to it themselves, and under a just God, will not long retain it!"

If we would sing, "Long may our land be bright with freedom's holy light" and mean it, if we would take the flame of freedom from the altars of our past and "secure the blessings of liberty for ourselves and our posterity...," we had better learn to distinguish the fire from the ashes!

II

A second, equally important fact is that—if we are to take the fire from the altars of our past, we must risk getting burned occasionally. Just as fire can be dangerous, freedom can sometimes be abused; it does not always work to our immediate advantage. That is why there are some who frankly (though mistakenly, I think), prefer benevolent tyranny. George Bernard Shaw once said, somewhat whimsically, I trust, that he "so passionately wanted efficient government of the people and for the people—that he could never accept government by the people!" He didn't want to risk the sometimes fumbling, slow and cumbersome methods of freedom.

It's certainly true that striving to preserve the flame of freedom—carries the risk of being burned, by inefficiency or worse: there'll always be irresponsible extremists who will use their freedom to deceive and mislead people, and there will be the possibility of traitors hiding behind constitutional guarantees of rights. These risks are inevitably inherent in a free society; but it's better to take the calculated risk than to accept the certain alternative of tyranny. Against the risk, of being singed by the fire of freedom, is the certainty of being suffocated in the ashes of authoritarianism!

And, if you have faith in people's capacity ultimately to recognize and respond to truth, you will believe as I do, that the only enduring political security is to be found in a society where a free exchange of opinions is maintained. As Thomas Jefferson once wrote: "In a democracy error by the majority may be tolerated as long as the minority is left free to correct it" This is the great genius and strength of a free society: its security rests upon the process, the maintenance of free expression—which can call attention to, and correct, its mistakes.

It is the dictatorship that is doomed to failure—because no one dares criticize its errors, which accumulate and eventually destroy it! Freedom functions like a refining fire: consuming falsehood and revealing truth. That is why it is so ironic that the self-designated super-patriots, in the name of "loyalty," would suppress the very freedom for dissent which has made and would keep our nation strong. It is patently stupid, as well as un-American, to say, "My country right or wrong." A democratic society depends upon its critics to correct its mistakes!

The greater danger to our nation (than the risks of freedom) was illustrated in a Herblock cartoon which depicted a man labelled "Hysteria" running up a ladder to the torch held by The Statue of Liberty. He is carrying a bucket of water and hollering "Fire!" Judge Learned Hand has memorably summarized the point:

> *Risk for risk, I'd rather take the chance that*
> *some traitors will escape detection—than spread*

abroad a spirit of general suspicion and distrust...I believe that a community is already in process of dissolution where each person begins to eye his neighbor as a possible enemy: where non-conformity is a mark of dis-affection; where denunciation... takes the place of evidence; where orthodoxy chokes freedom of dissent; where faith in the eventual supremacy of reason has become so timid that we dare not enter our convictions in the open lists, to win or lose. Such fears as these are a solvent which can eat out the cement that binds the stones together; they will, in the end, subject us to a despotism as evil as any that we dread...The mutual confidence upon which all else depends can be maintained only by an open mind and a brave reliance upon free discussion.

In short: if we are to take from the altars of our past the fire of freedom, we will risk getting burned occasionally, but that is preferable to the alternative of tyranny. And, in the long run, freedom carries its own fire insurance!

III

My last point has two parts, both of which are illustrated by a story: Years ago the rising waters behind one of the great dams in the Tennessee Valley were threatening to engulf a very old log cabin. A new home had been built for the family on a location safely above the high water mark, but the people had refused to move. Investigation disclosed that their reluctance was caused by the fire on the hearth of the log cabin. "My grandpa built that fire a hundred years ago," the man explained. "He never let it go out—for he had no matches, and it was a long trip to the neighbor's. When grandpa died, my pa tended that fire and since he died, I've tended it, and none of us ever let it die! And I ain't gonna move away and let Grandpa's fire go out!" Well, the engineers brought a large, iron kettle, gathered up the coals in the old fireplace, and carried them to the new house, where fresh kindling was added. And so, the family was able to move from their shack in the valley to the new home on the hill and take with them the fire of their ancestors.

All of which is to say, first of all, that a container is necessary to carry the fire of freedom into a new generation, a context for the living flame. There is no freedom apart from responsibility: no liberty without community. For freedom to function requires a framework of recognized obligations. It is not license to anarchy, but as President Eisenhower once put it, "The precious privilege of self-discipline."

That is why The Constitution, aptly described as a "Declaration of Inter-dependence" had to follow the Declaration of Independence: to furnish a context of law in which our freedom could function responsibly: a container for the fire! Listen to its Preamble: "We, the people of the United States, in order to form a more perfect union, establish justice, insure domestic tranquility, and secure the blessings of liberty for ourselves and our posterity do ordain and establish this Constitution." (Someone once suggested that we ought to have a Statue of Responsibility on the west coast—to balance the Statue of Liberty on the east coast and remind us of the Constitutional context of our freedom. It is a worthy thought.)

The reason that the song, "America" includes the words, "confirm thy soul in self control, thy liberty in law..." is that whenever people do not exercise their freedom responsibly, they invite the curtailment of that liberty. Cries of outrage at "government interference with private enterprise" fail to recognize that, if farmers were treating migrant workers fairly, there would be no need for laws to protect the workers; if Black people weren't being discriminated against, there would be no need for civil rights legislation; if landlords weren't behaving irresponsibly there would be no need for rent control!

As Edmund Burke wrote almost 200 hundred years ago: "(We) are qualified for civil liberty in exact proportion to (our) disposition to put moral chains on (our) own appetites (translate that "greed"!). (People) of intemperate minds cannot be free; their passions (lacking self-restraint) forge their fetters." Carrying the flame of freedom from the altars of our past requires a container, a context of responsibility which, if not self-imposed, must be imposed by government.

But there was a second element in the story of "grandpa's fire": after the coals were carried to the new fireplace, "fresh kindling was added to the fire." Which is to say that, if we are to keep alive the flame of freedom from the altars of our past, we must continually replenish it with our own devotion.

"New occasions teach new duties," the Unitarian poet James Russell Lowell once wrote, observing wisely that freedom must be restated, reinterpreted and renewed by every generation. Like anything else alive, it must be constantly growing in its meaning, to be relevant for changing times. That is why John Gardner suggested that "the apprenticeship of liberty is unending," that "...the requirement of free society's survival is that each generation re-discover this truth."

I close with a story about a young girl who was taken to see the Statue of Liberty. It was a memorable experience for her, but that night she was unable to sleep. When her father asked what was the matter, the girl replied, "I'm worried about the big lady with the lamp. She must get awfully tired. Don't you think that someone ought to help her hold up the torch?" It's a homely story, but that's precisely the attitude that's needed. If our nation is to preserve the flame of freedom from the altars of its past, it will require the thoughtful, courageous, and responsible citizenship of people like you and me. To state the matter as plainly as I can: whenever you or I do not exercise our right to dissent in the face of social injustice, we, in effect, starve the flame of freedom's holy light!

The Holy War— Then And Now!

The United Nations Charter begins "We the people of the United Nations— determined to save succeeding generations from the scourge of war..." I want to examine what I think is the single, greatest obstacle to that objective: The "Holy War" mentality.

Warfare is as old as humankind. Since the beginning of civilization, people have fought one another for food, for land, for natural resources, and justified their aggression in terms of survival. But anyone who's studied history is aware of the fact that the most vicious wars were those fought in the name of religion, sanctified destruction seems to know no boundaries of decency.

I will review the historical phenomenon of The Holy War, analyze the mentality which produces such barbaric behavior, and point out that there are those among us today, who seem intent upon fomenting such a mentality: people who must be clearly identified for the warmongers that they are!

I   An Historical Review

The first, major manifestation of The Holy War was that fought by Christians and Moslems; it was called "The Crusades" and lasted from the beginning of the 7th until the end of the 17th centuries. Depicted in our history books and Hollywood films as a glorious adventure of noble knights in armor, the Crusades were actually a grisly business.

Setting out from France under the banner of the Cross (symbol of "The Prince of Peace") those "righteous" warriors began by beating and burning Jews and destroying their synagogues; then they marched across Europe, plundering and ravaging their way to Jerusalem.

On the 15th of July, in 1099, the Crusaders entered "The

Holy City," went to The Church of the Holy Sepulcher, knelt before the tomb of Christ to bless themselves, and then proceeded systematically to slaughter every Moslem they could find! Men, women, children, old and young alike were killed until, according to their own accounts, the Via Dolorosa (where Jesus had borne the cross) was literally flowing with blood! The butchery was justified on the grounds that these people were unbelievers who desecrated The Holy land with their presence and represented the "anti-Christ" of Biblical prediction, which would rise up and destroy the world if it were not itself exterminated. As indicated earlier, these Crusades constituted nearly 1100 years of intermittent warfare, cost the lives of two million people. and finally ended when both sides realized that neither would prevail: they would have to learn to live together.

The next, great religious war was fought between the Christians themselves. Again, our popular history books tend to depict The Reformation as a polite theological debate, but the fact is that it launched 200 years of ruthless warfare: Catholics and Protestants mutilated, tortured and murdered each other with a frenzy of hatred that only accompanies a Holy War view of the "enemy" as evil incarnate. In this instance the Roman Church saw Martin Luther as "the anti-Christ," while Reformers viewed the Pope himself as fulfilling that role. Each side, therefore, thought of itself as serving a sacred cause: the extermination of an un-redeemable evil. Both finally fell back in exhaustion to recognize that they would have to learn to live together in this world.

By the 18th century many thoughtful people believed that they had seen the last of religious wars. Conflicts continued, of course, but they were carried on by professional soldiers, armies which observed certain rules of civilized warfare. As one historian put it, "England and France were at war thirty-five minutes out of every hour during the 18th century, but there was no obsessive hatred of one people for another." In the midst of such conflict it was still possible for one culture to admire the philosophy, literature and art of the other. And so, in the 19th century, The Holy War became regarded as a thing of the primitive past, neglecting the fact that religious fanaticism is capable of assuming many forms.

At that time the modern cult of nationalism emerged as the effective religion for most of the people of the world. It has, of course, persisted and thrived. Throughout the earth today, it is the reverent feeling of national-faith which evokes the deepest sense of belonging, the greatest sense of commitment and loyalty, the strongest willingness to fight and kill if necessary, to protect the sacred honor of that political-faith entity.

World War I was the first illustration of this new kind of religious conflict. Ten million human beings were killed when supposedly civilized people: British, French, German, Italian, Austrian, Russian, and finally American—fell upon each other with a fury far out of proportion to the issues being disputed. Each was willing to believe the vilest stories about the other and behave in ways that fulfilled their foes' fantasized fears. It is impossible to account for the intensity of the hatred exhibited in that war, especially between the British and the Germans (whose monarchs were cousins), unless you recognize it as reflecting the fervor of a religious fanaticism, of which nationalism was simply the latest manifestation. A more obviously obsessive expression of the phenomenon can be identified in the rise of Nazism in Germany, where propaganda techniques were developed and used so brilliantly to foment a sense of divine destiny: to conjure up a "sacred mission" to conquer the "non-Aryan world," beginning with the extermination of Jews.

The next great event in the evolution of The Holy War mentality was engendered by the emergence of the Communist ideology at the end of World War I. Clearly another expression of secular religion, Communism had its sacred writings, its dogma and true believers, its evangelists and martyrs, and a characteristic intolerance of differing faiths or dissidents within its own. Of course, the metaphysical base was atheistic, but psychologically Communism (and the anti-Communism it usually engenders) bears all the traits of a fervent religious fanaticism, the kind which fuels the fires of Holy War. Which leads us to a review of the mentality of the religious warrior:

II   The Holy War Mind-Set

There are three facets of Holy War fanaticism which I would focus upon — (manifestations of them in current thinking should be obvious): The first is that Holy War crusaders have always believed that theirs was a divine mission: that "God is on their side." The belt buckles of German soldiers said it explicitly: "Gott mit uns!" (Communists of course, would leave "God" out of it and talk instead of History being on their side, but the effect is the same: that of feeling self-righteously sanctified in their plunder.

With this mind-set, those who oppose you are seen as not merely your enemies but the enemies of God and everything that is holy. Therefore, anything you have to do, however immoral under ordinary circumstances, is justified by the righteousness of the cause. That of exterminating such satanic evil. A concomitant belief is that any ally in that cause is automatically good, whatever immoralities that nation may be guilty of. Moral absolution is conferred as a reqard for their allegiance.

And so, Christians slaughtered Moslems with Holy zeal, and the Moslems, understandably, reciprocated. And, when the savage Mongols, under Genghis Khan, swept out of Asia to attack the Islamic nations, the Pope received their emissaries as "friends." Though they shared little else, they shared a common enemy, and that was anough. And during World War II, when the Russians were fighting with the allied forces against Nazi fascism, they were "good guys," but, when that war was over, they became the "God-less enemy," and, instead of talking about "the Prussian military mentality," we began to refer to "the Slavic mind" as being "incapable of understanding any language but the language of force."

A second, related dimension of the Crusader mentality is the belief that the "enemy" is so diabolically evil that he is incapable of responding to any gesture of reason and goodwill. In psychological terms, our characterization of our foes as evil incarnate allows us to engage in "projection" i.e. attributing to the enemy the basest impulses of our own nature: civilization has taught us to suppress. (Indeed, some suggest impulses toward hate and destruction that this is why we need "enemies.")

And so, Holy Warriors fashion all kinds of fantasies and fasten them upon their foes. Christians saw Moslems as idolatrous, sexually licentious and inherently violent people, just as the Moslems viewed them! (and as Catholics and Protestants, British and Germans, Communists and anti-Communists have seen each other.) In recent years fundamentalist Christians have elevated all this into a pious, parlor game of identifying the current enemy with "The Beast of the Apocalypse," or the anti-Christ of Biblical prophecy. The practice sets up:

The third element in the Holy War mentality is that of seeing the "enemy" as such a powerful force of evil that, if we do not destroy them, they will destroy us. In short, there is no co-existence with such monstrous bestiality; it is our "sacred responsibility" to eradicate it from the face of the earth.

Christians and Moslems believed this of each other, and then, when Genghis Khan (of all people) finally persuaded them to sit down at a peace conference, they discovered to their astonishment that they had much more in common with each other, theologically as well as culturally, than either did with the Mongols. Later, Pope Pius XII was to describe the Crusades as "simply a difference between two forms of monotheism," a difference which took 1100 years and two million lives to settle!

My fear is that we won't have 1100 years to fight the next Holy War. It'll be over in eleven minutes, and almost everyone on this planet will probably die! The rest will wish they had! —Which leads to my last point:

III   The "Beast" is the Paranoia

There are those in our society (as there are in Russia, China, and other nations) who tend to generate the mentality of The Holy War: fomenters of a fanatical hatred who must be identified for what they are or they will stir up a frenzy of fear and distrust that could result in the destruction of our world. If you want to conjure up a deadly beast of apocalyptic dimensions, it is that Holy War mentality itself which deserves that designation!

Let me not be misunderstood; I am not suggesting that evil should be ignored. I applaud any effort to put morality into our foreign policy: to criticize and withhold financial aid from nations which violate basic, human rights, especially if that policy is even-handedly applied. Nor am I proposing a naive, unilateral disarmament, which would fail to recognize the realities of military might in our imperfect world.

What I am condemning is the hatriotism of those who would depict us as the divinely appointed guardians of Truth and Righteousness, with a holy calling to annihilate a so-called "Godless enemy." It is the kind of pseudo-religious fanaticism I hear in the statements of the spokesmen of the military-industrial-complex, who have a billion-dollar vested interest in fomenting such attitudes.

It is that kind of war-mongering paranoia I read in Alexander Solzhenitsyn's book, "Warning to the West" with his words about our being "in the dragon's belly," a clear allusion to The Beast of the Apocalypse and a revival of the myth of Communism's being a monolithic monster that threatens to devour us all. (The fact is that modern Communism is no more monolithic than Capitalism is.) It is that kind of deliberate misrepresentation of the realities of our modern world which is always in danger of gaining popular acceptance in our nation, especially when people are feeling insecure and need scapegoats. A Californian, Clifford Turner, captured The Holy War mood of many people in this bit of verse:

> Hush my children. Now be still. We have lots of overkill.
> We can kill them twenty times: they can kill us only seven.
> If they kill us seven times, all of us will go to heaven.
> If we kill them twenty times, and we can do it very well,
> They have done so many crimes, all of them will go to hell!
> Children, do not make a fuss. It should really comfort us

That when we get into a fight, we are absolutely right.
But they have done so much that's wrong, hell is where they all belong.

One of the first persons to recognize the stupid futility, as well as the immorality of the Crusades, was Francis of Assissi. He asked his Christian contemporaries, "Do you not realize that Moslems also are human beings?" I would suggest that we would do well to remember that Communists, too, are human beings, with no more, innate capacity for evil than we have. Most people who live in Communist lands did not choose that philosophy of government, any more than we chose to be born in this country. But those who did choose that ideology, did so because they sincerely believed that it best served their personal and national interests.

Herblock, the political cartoonist, once depicted a global scene with a portly American looking across the ocean at a starving couple peering into a trash can for food. The trash can was labelled "Communism," and the caption below had the American saying, "How can they eat that stuff?" The answer, of course, is that "they eat that stuff" because they're hungry and there's nothing else to eat! The Cubans chose Communism because it promised them something better than they had known under the dictatorship of Batista. The Chinese chose Communism in preference to the oppression they experienced under Chiang Kai-shek.

The Vietnamese chose Communism rather than economic exploitation by the French. And in each of these instances, our government had been supporting the corrupt, oppressive rulers. Those peoples' distrust of us—is understandable.

For our nation now to view them with paranoid hatred—is a sign of weakness, not strength; it is more pointedly a projection of our own guilt. To say we must destroy them because of their political ideology is to trumpet our moral bankruptcy to the world. Most importantly, it is a prelude to cataclysmic conflict. Let us be done with such Holy War mentality, lest it bring on the Armageddon we fear.

The Dream of a World United...

When The League of Nations collapsed, Woodrow Wilson, who had given so much of himself to that endeavor, commented, "The dream of a world united against the waste of war— is too deeply imbedded in the human heart— ever to be completely defeated." That is the way I like to think of The United Nations: as the long-delayed flowering of a dream: the global expression of an ideal which began to evolve when primitive people first tried to live cooperatively, instead of fighting each other for food, shelter and dominance. Indeed I would suggest that it is a dream whose evolutionary development is reenacted in the social growth of every human being.

Let me approach the matter by telling you about a biological theory which contends that "ontogeny recapitulates phylogeny." The idea is not really as complicated as that mouthful of syllables makes it sound. It merely suggests that the ontogenetic process (i.e. the development of the human embryo) recapitulates or reenacts the drama of phylogeny, the historic evolution of phyla (the classes of animal life). In other words, every human being (including you and me) experienced, in our prenatal states, a reenactment of the drama of evolution. Beginning as one-celled animals, we became more complex, passed through a fish-like stage, an amphibian existence, and so forth until finally, we reached the physical form of a human being and birth.

This theory has always fascinated me, not only because of its biological significance (which must really confound the "creationists!") but because it has other intriguing applications, the most relevant here being that human beings also reenact, in our social development, the historic evolution of the capacity for interpersonal relationship.

At birth, a human infant is really nothing more that an

animal, a delightful creature, especially in its parent's eyes, but creature none-the-less (as someone described, "an alimentary canal with lungs"!) And then the great day comes when, its eyes having learned to focus and its mind experiencing recognition, the baby bursts forth with its first, real smile. The significance of that first smile is momentous because with it and through it, the infant is registering its initial experience of conscious relationship. And that, I believe, is the beginning of human personality development. (The crossing of a threshold from an animal to a personal existence.)

As the child grows, socially, he or she cultivates a wider and wider range of relationships: first, the members of the family, then the other families in the neighborhood, then a school community, the home town, the state, the nation—until, when fully mature, a sense of relatedness to the whole of humankind! In doing this the child re-lives the drama of human, social development: the historic evolution of: the family, the gathering of families into a tribe, the assembling of tribes into a state, the federation of states into a nation, and finally, the achievement consummated in 1945, a recognition of the interdependency of all human beings, with the formation of The United Nations.

Centuries ago, some of the dimensions of this dream were given voice by the prophet Isaiah, who spoke of a world in which "swords shall be beaten into plowshares...where each shall sit under his vine tree and none shall make them afraid." And every, major religious teacher since that time, has echoed this longing and exalted "the dream of a world united against the waste of war."

More recently, the social scientists (psychologists like Erich Fromm and Eric Berne, and sociologists like Pitrim Sorokin and Ashley Montagu) have identified the source of the dream as something embedded in the human heart. (As Robert Frost put it in a poem, "Something there is that does not love a wall, that wants it down.") What modern studies of human nature are saying is that there is a deep hunger in the human heart (not only a capacity for but) a hunger for—relationship: a yearning which drives boys and girls into gangs, men and women into clubs (and churches), the same impulse-need which prompted a little child to push notes through an orphanage gate which read, "Whoever finds this, I love you." The United Nations is simply the final, full expression of their longing for interdependent relationship. Many things might be said about this matter; I will limit my observations to three:

I

The first—is somewhat negative but must be said. What has been, throughout history, the noble dream of isolated, prophetic voices, has now become sheer necessity, the stern requirement of survival! The world has become too small for anything but cooperation, too dangerous for anything but peace. Some time ago I saw a cartoon depicting a robed pilgrim carrying a placard which read: "Love thy neighbor for ten full days. If not fully convinced..." In short, give it a try; what can you lose? More appropriate in recent years is another cartoon which shows two men carrying signs that say, "Repent for the judgment day is at hand," and the caption has one of them commenting, "I like to see the expression on their faces when I glance at my watch!"

Well, people have talked of doomsday for years, and heretofore they've been dismissed as fanatics. But we've now reached a circumstance in human history where Armageddon is a very real possibility. One 20-megaton, hydrogen bomb, standard equipment on our planes— as well as those of the Soviet Union, is equal in explosive power, to ALL the bombs dropped in World War II. And there are thousands of them on this planet!

A few years ago, when there was talk about developing a "clean bomb," I came across this bit of verse: "To call the H-bomb clean/ makes sound and sense divergent/ unless of course it's meant to mean/ The Ultimate detergent!" (That's like calling the MX missile, "The Peacemaker!") The fact is that more and more nations are in possession of such ultimate weapons of destruction, and, unless the United Nations succeeds, one of them, surely, is going to use them!

Years ago, when the atomic cannon was unveiled at Aberdeen, Maryland, a truck full of American soldiers, returning from the event, were heard singing the familiar

"Whiffenpoof Song." The words, on this occasion, had a haunting poignance: "We're poor little lambs who have lost our way, Baa Baa Baa. Little black sheep who have gone astray...Baa Baa Baa. Gentlemen songsters off on a spree, doomed from here to eternity. Lord have mercy on such as we...Baa Baa Baa."

The tragic irony of our situation is that the technological developments, which make the modern world so dangerous, also hold promise of a world of economic abundance: where the basic necessities of life are available to every human being. We are like Damocles, who sat before a sumptuous banquet feast but, because there was—over his head—a sword, suspended by a single hair, he was afraid to stir and partake of the food. So, we sit under the threat of nuclear war, paralyzed by our fears and unable to enjoy and share the fruits of our technology.

Instead, we frantically stockpile bigger and better bombs while half the world goes to bed hungry every night! President Eisenhower once said of The United Nations, "Never before in history has so much hope for so many—been gathered in a single organization." Today we must add the paraphrase, "Never before has so much terror for so many been promised— if The U.N. fails." What was once a noble dream has become stern necessity—for the survival of the human race.

II

The second thing I would say—is that, if this dream is to be fulfilled, it will require greater men and women than the world has known before: people with larger vision and a capacity for commitment to that awareness. Sir Thomas Beecham, the orchestra conductor, once said that Mozart's "Don Giovanni" has never had an adequate performance. He meant that there never had been, at one time in any one place, performers capable of doing justice to the composer's demanding score: the vision had yet to be fulfilled in human endeavor. So it is with the political ideal of The United Nations: its realization will require a new breed of men and women, wiser and more mature human beings, capable of the imaginative understanding and emotional strength needed to render the promise of that dream. Patrick Henry reflected the kind of maturity and wisdom I have in mind when, in the early days of our own nation, he said to The Continental Congress, "The distinctions between Virginians, Pennsylvanians and New Englanders—are no more. I am not a Virginian but an American!" We, too, are going to have to recognize that affirming allegiance to a larger union of people, which projects the same ideals as those of our own nation, is not disloyalty to our native land. The long range interests of each of the nations, including our own, and the best interests of The United Nations— are one!

By the same token, we will have to exhibit an emotional strength that enables us to be sensitive instead of scared selfish, creative rather than rigid in our responses to the difficult demands of our day. It takes a strong sense of personal security to see the real enemies: the hunger, disease and abject misery of millions, and not be driven back by the ugliness of that sight. The fulfillment of the dream, represented in The United Nations, will require wisdom and maturity from the leadership of the major powers in the world. And it's up to those of us, who are citizens of those nations and care about humanity, to demand such wisdom and maturity from our leaders! To cite a specific example: our government cannot refuse to accept the jurisdiction of the World Court when we don't like its judgments. And those of us who recognize the wrongness of such a stance should say so, loudly and clearly.

III

There is, however, one more comment I must make, which stems from a realization that the people in power may not be equal to the challenge at this time: that the dream of a world united against the waste of war— may be beyond the current capacities of human character. My urgent insistence is that *that* possibility (that The United Nations might fail) must not deter us! It is better to fail in such a worthy endeavor that will someday succeed (because it must! even if it has to be resurrected from the ashes of an incinerated earth) than to abandon the dream imbedded in the human heart and thereby betray humanity and ourselves.

At the time of The U.S. Senate hearings on ratification of The U.N. Charter, Senator Vandenberg of Michigan aptly said, "You may tell me that I have but to scan the present world with realistic eyes to see these fine phrases reduced to shambles, that some of the signatories to this charter practice the precise opposite of what they preach, that the aftermath of this war seems to threaten the disintegration of these ideals at the very moment they are born. I reply that the nearer right you may be in such a gloomy indictment, the greater is the need for a new pattern which promises at least to try to stem these evil tides. If the effort fails, we can at least face the consequences with clean hands!"

I'll simply say "Amen" to that: whatever the immediate outcome of our endeavor, The United Nations Dream is worthy of our whole-hearted devotion. It is, as are all moral choices in the final analysis, a matter of self-affirmation. As Howard Thurman once wrote! We must "Keep alive the dream in the heart...for as long as we have a dream in our hearts, we cannot lose the significance of living."

V

PSYCHOLOGICAL SUGGESTIONS

Trust Your Tears

Then a woman said, Speak to us of Joy and Sorrow. And he answered:
Your joy is your sorrow unmasked. And the self-same well from which your laughter rises was oftentimes filled with your tears.
And how else can it be?
The deeper that sorrow carves into your being, the more joy you can contain.
Is not the cup that holds your wine the very cup that was burned in the potter's oven? And is not the lute that soothes your spirit, the very wood that was hollowed with knives?....
Some say, 'Joy is greater than sorrow.' Others say, 'sorrow is the greater.'
But I say unto you, they are inseparable.
Together they come, and when one sits lone with you at your board,
remember that the other is asleep upon your bed. Verily you are suspended like scales between your sorrow and your joy.
Only when you are empty are you at standstill and balanced.
—from "The Prophet" by Kahlil Gibran

In a museum in Jerusalem there is a display case which contains a collection of tiny cups. When asked what they were for, the guide explained that the little, ceramic goblets were sacramental vessels. But they were not employed in public religious ceremonies; they were for private, personal use. People cried into them. At times of great sorrow or great joy, when a flood of tears came forth, they were caught and kept on the mantle of a home. What the original owners of the cups seem to be saying—is that tears are precious:

they show that you care. And we should remind ourselves of the times we cared so deeply about something that we wept greatly.

Well, in a society where "caring enough means to send the very best Hallmark cards," I suggest that it would be well for us to learn from those ancient Jews to treasure our tears.

I

I address this matter because there is a tendency, in our culture, to distrust our tears: to trivialize and suppress them. Think about the last time you cried. How did you feel about it? Most people are embarrassed and seek to stifle the flow as quickly as possible. Every minister has counseled persons whose troubles warrant great sorrow and copious crying. But when the tears come, they apologize for "breaking down," sigh deeply to suppress the tears, and strive mightily to "compose themselves."

Why do we do this? We all do. We men have a particularly hard time expressing our deep sorrows, or our moments of great joy, with weeping. That's why we're more prone to heart attacks! We all resist crying because we're afraid of our feelings. We don't want to lose control. We don't want to appear weak. And sometimes we don't want to risk the vulnerability of caring that much.

Our fearful fantasy is that, if we let go and allow the tears to flow, we'll never stop crying, that we'll do something foolish or self-destructive. But the reality is that nothing is more foolish and self-destructive than suppressed feeling. Our concern with appearing weak ignores the fact that those who stifle their feelings are truly weakened. The suppression of emotion leaves them bereft of the sources of power. Indeed, it is a sign of strength to be sensitive and caring and capable of expressing deep emotion. And vulnerability, which literally means "susceptible to being wounded," is an index of aliveness. Only those who never love—never risk the loss of a loved one. Only those who never feel, avoid the pain of suffering. Only those who have never lived, avoid the sorrow of dying.

May Sarton, in a poem entitled "Control," describes

another consequence of totally suppressing our strong emotions. It begins:

> Hold the tiger fast in check
> Put the leash around his neck.
> Make it known a growl will tighten
> The collar. Browbeat. Frighten.
>
> Set the tiger on a tightrope.
> Make him walk it, make him cope.
> Punish any slightest fumble.
> Make him walk it, watch him tremble.

Then she concludes, two stanzas later,

> Tame the tiger. Break his pride.
> You will find yourself outside
> With all those who can destroy
> Tiger love and tiger joy.
>
> Outside in the awful dark,
> Smothered every smallest spark
> Where nothing blesses or can bless,
> How will you bear the loneliness?

Some of you have probably heard of Father Damien, the Catholic priest who went to Molokai to live with the lepers. For 13 years he worked with them as a friend and spiritual counselor. You may also know that Father Damien eventually contracted leprosy and died from it. But you may not know the circumstances under which he discovered that he had the disease. One morning he spilled boiling water on his foot and didn't feel it! That's when he knew he was doomed. So, if you have not recently felt tears of sorrow and regret in this anguished world, do not congratulate yourself. The absence of pain is no proof of the presence of health. It may be the evidence of a loss of sensitivity which is a form of death!

II

My contention is that we must learn to treasure and trust our tears for they have much to teach us. I will focus on three things we will discover.

The first is that life is essentially tragic, not merely often unfair, but intrinsically tragic! We don't want to believe this. We rebel against it and sometimes our noblest acts spring from such rebellion. But as someone wrote, "For those who think, life is comic. For those who feel, life is tragic."

A little girl, standing on a curb and looking at a mud-puddle in which an oil slick was making iridescent colors, once said, "Oh, look mother, there's another rainbow gone to smash." Life is like that. It's a weird mixture of happiness and heartache, of triumphs and failures, of high hopes and rainbows "gone to smash." And somewhere on our way to mature adulthood, we recognize that all our triumphs are transitory, all our satisfactions are temporary, all our relationships are imperfect and even then subject to sudden termination. It is a given, built into the nature of human consciousness, that our intellectual "reach exceeds our grasp," that we yearn for that which can never be fully realized, that death is the ultimate manifestation of the fact that there are no permanent victories.

Walt Whitman once wrote of animals, "They do not lie awake in the dark and weep..." Of course not. They're animals, who live without the blessing and curse of human consciousness. The high hazard of being human, the deepest spring from which our tears flow, is an awareness of the vast gulf between what we can imagine and what life is. But when we tearfully recognize that this existential condition is something we share with every other human being, a bond of kinship can be established that makes life not only bearable, but sometimes even joyous. (Which leads to my second observation.)

Our tears can teach us what really matters. They're often the saline solution which clears our eyes to life's enduring values. Indeed, we cry when we are confronted with either the loss of, or a beautiful, moving expression of, that which we most value. So, crying is always revealing of what matters most to us. If you want to know what you truly prize, keep a diary of your deepest disappointments and highest joys. For to paraphrase Jesus, "where your treasure is, there will be your tears also." And what are the values that most often evoke the tears of joy and sorrow? An African

Pygmy Chief, named Kitabu, once eloquently expressed them:

> If you give a piece of your heart to things that you own, you cannot love people with all of your heart. You become the slave of the things that you own. We love and take care of people, not things. The whites think we are poor. Let them think what they please! Happiness is the smile on the face of your wife when you bring home the antelope. Happiness is the laughter of your children. Happiness is the music you make. Happiness is freedom. These are not things that you own—they are things you enjoy.

Another reflection of what really matters in life was written by Roland de Pury, the minister of a small church in Lyons, France, during the Nazi occupation of that country. One summer morning in 1942, he was seized and taken to prison for eight months. Shut in a cell by himself, the door locked and even the small window covered, he later wrote,

> I was alone. My only way out was a door I could not open. I would gladly have chosen to be beaten, starved, or tortured—if it would but permit me 15 minutes conversation with a human being.

Eight months after that fateful Sunday, the door opened. His name was called. He was to be freed on a prisoner exchange. He descibes his first meal in the world of the living:

> The words of Thanksgiving before that meal were no mere formality - but the stammering of men drunk with pure gratitude...I went up to my room. My room, not my cell. Then I opened and shut the door - and opened and shut the door - and opened and shut the door again. I was rich! I staggered with the wealth of a door that would open under my own hand.

Our tears can teach us what matters in life.

And finally, our tears can drive us to discover the deeper sources of comfort available to every human being. The word comfort, from the Latin "cum forte," literally means "with strength." And there is, deep inside every one of us, a strength greater than we ever dreamed, a strength which is only discovered when we are driven to the extremities of feeling.

For such strength comes not in response to a solicitous soothing that would shelter us from life's tragic dimensions. It is most evoked, from the recesses of our own being, when we are challenged to break out of the prison of self-centered sorrow and demonstrate to the world that "death shall have no dominion" over our souls, nor shall any tragedy break our spirits.

My colleague, Robert Weston, once put it well,

Shall I tell you where there is comfort?
Not in the warm bed,
Nor at the table with food piled high;
Not in the promise that our tears shall be wiped away
And our wounds healed,
But that we weep for that which is worth weeping;
That our wounds were gained in warfare for a cause
Which shall live in the hearts of people when we are gone.
Who shall placidly offer praise
to God for blessings
While a child goes naked and hungry?

Comfort comes not down from the skies
But from the heart out.
And you shall not be comforted
Except by the knowledge that you have done what you could.

The ancient Jews were wise to treasure their tears. For they teach us that life is essentially tragic, that what matters most is truly loving relationships, that there is strength to be found in a sensitized awareness that calls us to greater caring and imperishable achievement. Trust your tears.

The Subtle Sin Of Self-Pity

When I was a theological student, serving my first congregation at the age of 22, one Sunday morning I announced that on the following week I would speak on the subject of "sin." After the service an elderly woman came over to me and said, with a kindly smile, "Son, you ain't lived long enough—to have sinned enough—to have repented enough—to be able to preach about it!" Well, I'm older now—and, reluctant as I am to claim any further qualifications, I want to discuss one of what I call "The Subtle Sins."

I regard self-pity as one of the most popular, non-pharmaceutical drugs in our society. I describe it as a narcotic because it's addictive, it gives momentary pleasure, and it separates us from reality! And can anyone doubt its prevalence? Can you honestly say that you've never felt sorry for yourself? If you think you can, submit yourself to the following tests (because self-pity sometimes manifests itself in very subtle ways!) Have you ever responded to the question "How are you?" with something like "Are you sure you've got time to listen?" Or have you ever brooded over one critical comment even though it was received in the midst of several complimentary ones? Or have you ever felt misunderstood or misjudged—and helpless to do anything about it? I've experienced all of these moods, and I suspect that you have also. So, let us examine three questions: Why do we engage in self-pity? What happens when we do? and How can we deal with this tendency?

I

At the most obvious and superficial level we indulge the practice because it is a soothing, psychological balm, a kind of pain relief. It is so comforting to feel "put upon" and so much easier to take refuge in the self-administered solace of feeling abused than to deal directly with the frustrations and disappointments we all encounter. Someone once wrote: "Hatred is the coward's revenge for being intimidated." That's true: we hate those with whom we feel powerless to deal. Similarly, self-pity is a safer, even sordidly satisfying way of responding to insult and injury when we're not able to respond directly, e.g. "The situation is hopeless; poor me, there's nothing I can do!" How soothing to be able to sink into the sighs of self-pity and be thereby relieved of responsibility! (Our motto might be: "If at first you don't succeed, sigh, sigh, again.")

It can even be pleasurable to get hooked on the habit of feeling sorry for ourselves: because it expands our sense of significance, it enlarges our feeling of importance to think we are so terribly abused and misunderstood. The language of the children's chant is indicative: "Nobody loves me, everybody hates me. I'm gonna eat worms and die." (And then, of course, they'll be sorry!)

Self-pity characteristically employs such cosmic language: "nobody, everybody; never, always; nothing I do, everything I say." Such sweeping generalizations serve to enlarge the significance of self. I experienced the lure of this kind of thinking several years ago. I had taken a public stand on a controversial issue and was being criticized by some members of the Congregation, which prompted one of my admirers to send along, as a gesture of encouragement, the following quotation by Ernest Hemingway,

> *If people bring so much courage to the world, the world has to kill them to break them, so, of course, it kills them. The world breaks everyone and afterward many are strong at the broken places. But those it will not break, it kills. It kills the very good and the very gentle and the very brave, impartially.*

How gratifying to receive such a tribute, but what a temptation to self-pity! How enticing the thought that, because I had been misunderstood, I must be good and brave. It would be easy to become addicted to such a rationalization of reality, and so comforting to believe that greatness can thus be so easily achieved. But, of course, the fact is that being maligned does not necessarily mean that you belong with the great martyrs of human history. That's merely the illusion fostered and enjoyed by those who indulge in "The Subtle Sin of Self-Pity." It *is* a soothing psychological drug!

II

Now to the second question: What happens as a result of this tendency? Why do I call it a "sin"? (My definition of sin is anything which is destructive of human welfare and human values.)

First, and again most obviously, self-pity dissipates our energies in negative, useless, indeed distortive activity, which eventually erodes and destroys identity. Let me approach the matter this way: life is growth. Anything which is alive is growing. And the essential ingredients of growth include a creative response to challenge. Thus, when human beings avoid the frustrations of experience, they abandon its growth-producing opportunities and fail really to live! We all experience pain, hurt, disappointment, grief etc., and to feel the hurt is healthy: sharing the grief can cleanse and clarify and heal. But to get stuck there, to wallow in the mire of self-pity is to consign ourselves to an early, psychological death. And that's a "sinful" thing to do!

The second reason that self-pity is a sin is that is encourages irresponsibility, sometimes fostering terribly insensitive and cruel acts which are justified by our warped and magnified sense of injury. The more we feel "put upon," the more righteous our efforts at retaliation: ennobling the "hatred (which) is the coward's revenge for being intimidated." There are many examples: an old, familiar one is that of a husband "on the prowl" who begins his amorous approach to another woman with the line, "My wife doesn't understand me." (So common, it's become a cliche.) To project this on a larger screen: when Richard Nixon was defeated in the gubernatorial election in California and said to the press, "You won't have Dick Nixon to kick around any more," that should have been a tip-off that he was nurturing a resentment which could eventually result in irresponsible behavior. The more we feel sorry for ourselves, the more we magnify our sense of injury, until, we feel outraged and justified in all kinds of insensitive and callous treatment of others.

III

Now to the most difficult question: How can we deal with this tendency toward self-pity? It's always easier to describe than to prescribe. But in this instance, the matter is complicated by the fact that the inclination is rooted in a low sense of self-esteem which is a fundamental and sometimes insurmountable barrier to creative living.

R.D. Laing, the British psychoanalyst, wrote a book entitled "Knots" in which he describes the squirrel-cage kind of thinking which many of us engage in because of our lack of self-esteem. Here are some illustrations of the circular reasoning which defies solution:

"I'm ridiculous,"
"No, you are not."
"Well, then, I'm ridiculous to feel
ridiculous when I'm not."

And again:

"You must be laughing at me
for feeling you are laughing at me
if you're not laughing at me."

There's no question that cultivating a sense of self-worth is necessary in any endeavor to deal with self-pity. But let us focus upon more immediate remedies:

The first thing I would suggest has to do with perspective. We have to maintain a larger view of our lives so that the inevitable frustrations and disappointments don't seem so catastrophic, and therefore so conducive to self-pity. As one of my Mrs. Malaprop friends once delightfully put it: "If it's not fatal, I'll live through it." What profound wisdom in that whimsical remark. And how much healthier than the soothing balm of self-pity.

Of course, humor always helps us to keep perspective when dealing with the vicissitudes of life. Theresa of Avila (later sainted by the Roman Catholic Church) once made a journey with fifty of her nuns. They came to an unstable bridge in the midst of a frightening storm. The nuns prayed that the bridge would hold until they had gotten safely across, but it collapsed and the faithful women were plunged into the stream. After they fished each other out and stood shivering on the bank, their leader looked toward heaven in reproach and said, "If this is the way you treat your friends, it's no wonder that you have so many enemies!" Such a sense of humor helps us remember that, though something may go wrong, it's not the end of the world; there are still reasons for refusing to succumb to "The Subtle Sin of Self-Pity."

Another ingredient of healthy perspective is purpose. Someone has said that there are two ways of being lost: not knowing where you are and not knowing where you're going? If we are to avoid the pitfall of self-pity, we'd better have something to do, not just busy work but something significant to occupy our thoughts and energies. If we have really important concerns to fill our days, we won't have the time or the inclination to feel sorry for ourselves. Life is too brief to waste any of it in self-pity.

One last thing I must mention for the maintenance of perspective: we need continually to remind ourselves of those whose problems make ours seem trivial. In some places, India for example, the life expectancy is thirty-two years of age; four out of ten children die before they're twelve years old! There, and in several other nations, "yaws" disease cripples children for life. Fifty million suffer from it, with sores that eat into their flesh and bones. A fifteen-cent shot of penicillin would cure "yaws" in its early stages, but they don't have the fifteen cents! In similar vein, I recently learned of an International Organization of Artists, whose members number several thousand people, who have one thing in common: they paint with brushes held in their mouths because they have lost the use of their hands. Remembering the circumstances of these and other people closer to us, helps us to keep a proper perspective on our problems.

The second suggestion I would make applies even to "Byronic despair," the feeling that life is unbearably cruel and disappointing. It is reflected in this bit of verse:

su-I-sigh-dull why?ing;
over-dose of pain relief
deadly more than bombing raids
thy self-inflicted dis-belief;
who and what you are—
you choose!—however passively,
no matter how the fates conspire
you make/forsake your destiny.

In short, what you are you choose to be!

Now, I don't want to be misunderstood. There are obvious limitations to the idea, and there are those whose lives are terribly determined by their condition . As Bertand Russell once wrote, "Anyone who maintains that happiness comes wholly from within, should be made to spend 36 hours in rags in a blizzard without any food!" But most of us don't have to deal with that kind of determinism; we may not have control over all of the events which befall us, but we do have the final decision regarding how we will respond to those events.

Dr. Albert Ellis, the psychologist, once said, "There are no such things as 'needs'; there are only 'wants.' You say you need love? No. You want love. You say, 'Well, I need food.' No. You want food. 'Well, I need to survive.' No. You want to survive." This contention may not be absolutely true, but it certainly is profoundly true and a valid corrective to our habitual pose of helplessness. When we say we can't help the way we are, we need to be told that that's nonsense! We want to be the way we are, or else we would change. If we wallow in the mire of self-pity, it's because we enjoy making our lives an endless recitation of misery and misfortune.

Victor Hugo once made a haunting statement, "If you don't get what you want in life, perhaps you didn't want it badly enough, or you tried to bargain over the price." Again, maybe that's an overstatement (another 100 percent half right idea), but for most of us, most of the time, it's profoundly true! Recognizing that fact may help us avoid "The Subtle Sin of Self-Pity."

I want to close with a story which tells of a young man in a small village who was terribly envious of the revered sage of the community. He decided one day that he would demonstrate to the townspeople that he was wiser than the old man. Holding a sparrow in his hand, he challenged the sage saying, "Old man, is this bird dead or alive?" His intention was that if the wise one said "alive," he would crush the sparrow; if he said "dead," the young man would open his hand and allow the bird to fly away. The old man looked deeply into his eyes, saw the trickery there and replied, "It is as you will, my son; it is as you will." And so it is for each of us. To a great extent, at least, we choose what will be, and that choice is sometimes a matter of life or death. We decide whether we will wallow in "The Subtle Sin of Self-Pity" or respond more creatively to the disappointments and frustrations of life.

The Subtle Sin Of Sentimentality

On Mother's Day, 1953, as a very young, seminary-student minister, I delivered a sermon on "The Cobalt Bomb!" My rationale was that if anyone ought to be concerned about the development of nuclear weapons, the mothers of America should be. Well, it "went over like a bomb." The small New England congregation I was serving didn't think that such a subject was appropriate to the occasion. Now, you would think that I should have learned something during the past three decades, but, here I am risking your displeasure by talking about the sin of sentimentality on Mothers Day! It simply serves to illustrate the contention that "the more things change, the more they remain the same."

I shall follow a familiar pattern, asking three questions: Why do we engage in sentimentality? What happens when we do? and How can we overcome the tendency?

Before we go further, however, some definitions are in order: The dictionary defines "sentiment"—simply as feeling: something which is obviously natural and good, indeed essential to being fully human. Anyone who is incapable of feeling, unable to experience joy and sorrow or express tears and laughter, is more like a machine than a human being.

But "sentimentality" is defined (in my "official, unabridged" Webster's)—as "an excess of feeling." The crucial question thus becomes, "how do you know when a feeling is excessive" and you are indulging in sentimentality? I would offer this (unofficial, personally abridged Perrino's) definition for our use this morning: sentimentality is the substitution of feeling for appropriate, intelligent thought and action.

For example: when someone substitutes a lump in the throat and the phrase "my country, right or wrong" for thoughtful, intelligent patriotism, that's sentimentality. Or, when someone sings emotionally of "gentle Jesus, meek and mild" (that "he walks with me and he talks to me, and he tells me I am his own") and ignores the ethical demands of the Nazarene's message, that's sentimentality. (It would have prayer in the schools—while keeping them racially segregated.) And particularly pertinent to the national holiday being observed today, when someone seeks to make up for a year-round neglect of a maternal relationship with a sudden display of exaggerated affection, that's sentimentality.

I

Why do we indulge in such substitution of feeling for appropriate, intelligent action? All of us do, at least occasionally. Probably because it's easier than doing something about the matter, and it gives us a facsimile of concerned involvement, without any effort or risk.

Think about the times when you are most prone to sentimentality. My guess is that they occur when you are tired, or confused, or frightened (had too much to drink?) or are just too lazy to do more than emote over the issue. On those occasions it's so satisfying to be able to wring our hands in despair about the state of the world and feel that we have done something by our caring. ("Ain't it a shame" is the conversational game we play. "Isn't it awful" is another variation of it.)

It's also much more pleasant to be able to romanticize a relationship—rather than undertake the difficult task of genuine loving and deal with a real, living, independent human being whose needs and desires do not always coincide with our own. It's similarly comforting to revel sentimentally in the beauty of nature and not think about its dangerous and destructive dimensions, to feel piously confident that "God's in his heaven and all's right with the world..." rather than do what needs to be done to make life more just on this planet. In short, we indulge in sentimentality because it relieves us of the obligation toward endeavor, by substituting feeling for action; and when we are tired, confused, or anxious, that's an appealing alternative.

II

But my contention this morning is that it's a bad bargain. Indeed, defining "sin" as any behavior which is destructive of life, I would suggest that sentimentality is one of the more subtle sins.

I've already revealed one of the reasons for this appraisal. The poet, William Butler Yeats, put it this way, "The rhetorician would deceive his neighbors; the sentimentalist deceives himself." Because such self-deception diminishes our selves and distorts our vision of reality, Thomas Carlyle flatly declared that "The barrenist of all mortals is the sentimentalist." An illustration of the way that sentimentality distorts our understanding and diminishes our capacity for appropriate thought and action—is to be found in the story of a woman who was being tried for the murder of her husband. She was obviously guilty of the crime, but one juror held out for an acquittal. When someone asked the juror why she would not convict the defendant, she replied, "Oh, I felt so sorry for her. After all she was a widow."

Similarly, the passive irresponsibility of religious sentimentalty is reflected in this paraphrase of Jesus' parable of the "The Last Judgment":

> *I was hungry and you formed a discussion group to lament my plight. I was in prison and you debated the need for more law and order. I was naked and you were shocked at the immorality of my appearance. I was lonely and poor, and you told me mournfully about the balance of trade deficits. You seem so respectable in your church. But I'm still very hungry, and cold, and lonely, and poor.*

The writer, Voltaire, once said that most people "read of injustice, feel outrage, have their dinner, and go to sleep!" And, because such irresponsible sentimentality diminishes our humanity, I regard it as a "subtle sin."

It is also destructive of relationships: of marriages, and families, and even friendships—where love is sentimentalized instead of being recognized as the most demanding and difficult of human endeavors. The most obvious example, especially appropriate today, is the sentimentality with which parents often relate to their children. They're so cute: like little toys to dress and undress and play with and show off to their friends. The problem arises when these babies grow up—with thoughts and feelings and wills of their own. And sometimes their parents never get around to accepting them as persons, rather than objects. To do so requires giving up the sentimental attachment that would keep them little and adorable, and get down to the arduous effort of developing and maintaining genuine love relationships.

Well, you can supply additional examples, to demonstrate the fact that sentimentality is a "sin" because it is destructive of human personality. If we were to stop here and simply lament the tragic waste of sentimentality, we would merely illustrate the inclination to substitute feeling for appropriate, intelligent thought and action.

III

So, on to the more difficult task: how do we overcome this tendency? First of all, to the extent that confusion is the underlying cause, we can obtain a clearer, more realistic understanding of the issue confronting us. For example, I would enjoin parents to read regularly from "The Prophet" by Kahlil Gibran, the passage which says:

> *Your children are not your children*
> *They are the sons and daughters of life's longing*
> *for itself...*
> *You may give them your love but not your*
> *thoughts.*
> *For they have their own thoughts.*
> *You may house their bodies but not their*
> *souls...*
> *For their souls dwell in the house of*
> *tomorrow...*

And to couples, inclined by anxiety toward a sentimental, "moonlight and roses" view of love, I would recommend this statement by Anne Morrow Lindberg:

When you love someone you do not love them all the time, in exactly the same way. It is an impossibility. It is even a lie to pretend to. And yet this is exactly what most of us demand. We have so little faith in the ebb and flow of life, of love, of relationships. We leap at the flow of the tide and resist, in terror, its ebb. We are afraid it will never return. We insist on permanency, on duration, on continuity; when the only continuity possible, in life as in love, is in growth, in fluidity—in freedom, in the sense that the dancers are free, barely touching as they pass, but partners in the same pattern.

The poet, Rilke, expressed a similar thought:

*Once the realization is accepted
that even between the closest human beings
infinite distances continue to exist,
a wonderful living side by side
can grow up, if they succeed
in loving the distance between them
which makes it possible for each
to see the other whole against the sky.*

Another antidote to sentimentality is humor, which always puts things in perspective. This story illustrates an apt corrective to religious sentimentality:

It had been raining for a long time and there was flooding. A farmer was standing in his fields with water up to his ankles. A car came along and the people said, "You'd better get in and come with us, it's going to get worse." "No," said the farmer, "I put my trust in God."

Soon, the farmer was up to his waist in water. A boat came along and the people said, "You'd better get in and come with us, it's going to get worse." "No," said the farmer, "I put my trust in God."

Soon, the farmer was up to his neck in water.

From a helicopter, flying overhead, he was told to grab hold of the ladder because it was going to get worse. "No," said the farmer, "I put my trust in God."

So—the farmer drowned—and met God. "I put my trust in you. Why didn't you help me?" he said. "How can you say that" God replied, "I sent you a car and a boat and a helicopter. What more do you want?"

Well, that is a clever restatement of the old saying that "God helps those who help themselves..." and leads to my last, and perhaps most crucial point. One of the reasons that sentimentality is so deceptively destructive—is that the feeling, substituted for action, never gets outside of your self. It may swell up your sense of significance (as a facsimile of concerned involvement), but because it is so egocentric, the emotion consumes, rather than creates, life.

Let me reach for an analogy by suggesting that living is like breathing: the air must come in and go out, if we're to stay physically alive. Similarly, our feelings must be expressed in action, or they will suffocate us psychologically. And so, the most effective antidote to sentimentality is doing something with our feelings. Mustering our deepest resources of energy, we can rise above the fatigue, confusion and anxiety to act on our noblest ideals.

The best example perhaps (returning to my theme of 30 years ago), is that we can sentimentally lament the fact that the leaders of the two most powerful nations of the earth are currently standing opposite each other like a couple of gorillas, thumping their chests and bellowing their superiority, or we can speak out against such insanity. To paraphrase an old quotation: we can't do everything, but we can do do something, and what we can do, we must do—if we're to be saved from "The Subtle Sin of Sentimentality."

Go For It!

At the next vacancy for God, if I am elected I shall forgive last the delicately wounded who, having been slugged no harder than anyone else, never get up again, neither to fight back, nor to finger their jaws in painful admiration.

They who are wholly broken, and they in whom mercy is understanding, I shall embrace at once and lead to pillows in heaven. But they who are meek by trade, baiting the best of their betters with extortions of mock helplessness—I shall take last to love...and never wholly.

Let them all into heaven—I abolish Hell—but let it read over them as they enter: 'Beware the calculations of the meek, who gambled nothing, gave nothing, and could never receive enough.'
—John Ciardi

I want to introduce this subject with an illustration from the game of football. I do so with a realization that many of you don't know much about the sport. (e.g. some of you probably think that "split ends" are what happens to your hair when it's too dry!) The term also refers to football players who line up apart from the rest of the team—to run downfield for a pass. When I told a friend I might open the sermon with that quip and asked if he thought it might be offensive to some people, he responded with a sly smile, "I think you should go for it!"

The popular phrase did probably originate with football fans. When the home team has the ball at midfield, and it's 4th down with a few feet to go for another first down, the prudent thing to do is "punt" and put the opponents deep into their own territory. But the crowd will begin to chant,

"Go for it," urging the team to risk not making the short yardage and having to give up the ball. Cautious coaches will ignore the crowd and "play it safe." (Some actually calling plays by the computer!) But, for the fans, it's a much more exciting game when the team is willing to gamble. And they seem to demand such daring from athletes.

Indeed, at the 1984 Olympic games we witnessed the curious spectacle of Carl Lewis, a winner of four gold medals in track events, being booed by the crowd. Their displeasure resulted from the fact that Lewis, who cleared more then 25 feet in his first attempt at the long jump (enough to win the gold), refused to take his last two jumps in an effort to set a new, world record. Lewis was simply being prudent. He might have injured himself, and he wanted to conserve his energy for three more events awaiting his conquest. But the fans were disappointed; they wanted him to "Go for it", not simply to be content with winning the gold, but to risk and give his all in the quest for excellence. As one sports writer observed, "Jesse Owens would've gone for it on two broken ankles! He wouldn't leave a world record lying there."

Well, whether or not we agree with the crowd reaction to Carl Lewis, I would like to commend the "Go for it" mentality as a healthy stance on life. Now, I realize that it's probably another one of those 100% half right ideas, which needs the balance of its corresponding opposite: namely, "Look before you leap." But for most of us, who are all too prone to be prudent, it is a valid and valuable corrective.

I

I like the phrase, first of all, because it is positive. It assumes that we can, to some extent at least, take control of our lives and daring some improbable dream, make it happen. It reflects a theological conviction that "destiny is not a matter of chance but choice!" It exalts the significance of what psychologist Rollo May terms "intentionality": suggesting that we have no idea of what we can accomplish with our lives until we stretch, risk, and commit ourselves to some effort.

I want to illustrate this contention with a story told by Bob Richards, the Olympic decathalon gold medalist, in his book "Heart of a Champion." It begins in the early 1900's with Charley Paddock, who, as a boy, had one, burning ambition: to be an Olympic runner. He trained with intense determination, and in 1920, at Antwerp, Belgium, set a new world record in winning the 100 meters race at the Olympic games. When he returned to the States, Paddock travelled the country as a forceful speaker, expounding on the theme, "If you think you can, you can!" After a talk at a high school assembly in Cleveland, a spindley-legged, Black student came up to him, and in a voice quivering with emotion, said, "Mr. Paddock, do you think I could be an Olympic Champion, just like you?" Paddock replied, "Young man, if you really work for it and train hard, you can become an Olympic Champion." Well, that boy ran and ran and trained with singleness of purpose, and in 1936, at Berlin, Germany, won four gold medals at the Olympic games. His name, of course, was Jesse Owens.

But the story doesn't end there. Owens came home to Cleveland and similarly gave speeches to audiences of young people. And one day another Black youngster, who was so thin that his friends called him "Bones," came over to Owen's car and said shyly, "I'd sure like to be an Olympic champion like you, Mr. owens." Jesse reached out and put his hand in the boy's and repeated what he'd been told, "If you really work for it and train hard, you, too, can be an Olympic champion, son." It was at Wembly Stadium in 1948 that Harrison "Bones" Dillard won the 100 meters finals and tied Jesse Owen's Olympic record at 10.3 seconds. Now, you might say, "Well, that's one of those rare coincidences that'll probably never happen again. But I am here to say that it will happen again and again, when young men and women are inspired by a vision of what they can become and are willing to "Go for it" with wholehearted devotion.

One of the reasons that this is true is suggested in a quotation from the German philospher, Goethe:

...the moment one definitely commits oneself, the Providence moves too. All sorts of things occur to help....A whole stream of events that

*issue from that decision, raising in one's favor—
all manner of unforeseen incidents and meetings
and . . . assistance . . . Whatever you can do, or
dream you can, begin it. Boldness has genius,
power, and magic in it.*

II

The second reason I like the phrase is that it's light-heartedly realistic. When someone says, "Go for it," the clear implication is that you might not get what you go for, but that's okay; it's still worth the effort. And this, too, is a much-needed corrective to our typical timidity, which will only bet on a "sure thing", that's always got to be "number one."

Indeed, the fear of failure is one of the most pervasive and pernicious emotions of human experience. How many people must go to their graves with unfulfilled lives because they were afraid to attempt anything which might not be successful? Tom Robbins, in a book entitled "Even Cowgirls Get the Blues," speaks to that anxiety with this passage:

So you think you are a failure? Well, you probably are. What's wrong with that? In the first place, if you have any sense at all you must have learned by now that we pay just as dearly for our triumphs as we do for our defeats. Go ahead and fail. Embrace failure! Seek it out! Learn to love it That may be the only way any of us will ever be free.

I'd like to illustrate what I think he means with a personal reference. I frequently swim in the ocean, and one of the things I enjoy is "body surfing." I wait until a big wave comes along and just before it crests, I leap onto it, stroke for shore, and try to lie flat upon the churning water. If I can catch the wave just right, it's an exhilarating experience to be borne by the rolling water all the way to the beach. But the timing is crucial, and the fact is that I am successful only on every third or fourth effort. The relevant fact is that, when I miss, I simply get up and go back out to wait for the next, big wave. I thought the other day, "Wouldn't it be healthy if we could greet all of life's opportunities that way? When something promising comes along, "go for it," without a lot of overly-serious ego-involvement in whether we're successful or not, because, of course, there'll be other opportunities.

George Bernard Shaw once summarized the thought when he said,"A life spent making mistakes is not only more honorable but more useful than a life spent daring nothing." And, I must add, it's a lot more fun. That's why Mark Twain, when asked if he had done anything in his life that he regretted, responded "I only regret the things I didn't do!" So, Go for it. Anything worth doing—is worth doing badly, rather than not doing it at all! Which leads to my last point:

III

The crucial, remaining consideration is: what makes something worth going for? At the obvious extreme, if you're racing a locomotive to an intersection, to "Go for it" would be stupid. The risks are too great and the gain too insignificant. So, what are the things worth going for? I can't prescribe specifics which would be appropriate for all of you. But I can suggest some general guidelines. One of them is expressed in Carlos Castaneda's book, "The Teachings of Don Juan". It contends:

Anything is one of a million paths....Look at every path closely...and ask (yourself), "Does this path have heart?"...If it does, the path is good; if it doesn't, it is of no use....

But what makes a path have heart? Minimally, it is when it takes you out of the narrow confines of self-centeredness— toward self-fulfillment. That, clearly, is one of the fundamental paradoxes of human experience: only "those who lose their lives in some larger, worthy purpose shall find life!" Years ago a comedian told a joke which reflects the reality. He said, "Today my heart beat 103,369 times. My blood traveled 168 million miles. I breathed 23,040 times, I ate 3 pounds of food, drank 2.9 pounds of liquid. I perspired 1.43 pints, I spoke 4800 words, moved 750 major muscles and exercised 7,000,000 brain cells. Boy, am I tired!" Well, that's exactly what happens when we focus entirely on ourselves. We get tired and depressed.

To put it another way: ours is a society literally dedicated to the pursuit of happiness, and pursue it we do: up the ladders of fame and fortune, down glittering streets and dark alleys, into department stores, theaters, and sports stadia, spending millions of dollars on gadgets, amusement, and ostentatious comfort, and then millions more on tranquilizers—to escape the emptiness of it all. But the fact is that there is no tranquilizer made that can quiet the restlessness of a life devoid of meaning. And, sooner or later, we must deal with the deeper longings of our heart if we're to find real joy. And that's something worth going for!

IV

In closing I'd like to point out that meteorologists have discovered that the hurricanes which strike the eastern coast of the United States are born in the Atlantic Ocean in the calm, warm, moist air of a region near the equator which is called "the doldrums!" (yes, called "the doldrums"?) Now, I always thought that "the doldrums" referred to a mood which all of us suffer from occasionally. But how much more meaningful the expression becomes when the metaphor is understood. So, "Go for it", go for some worthy objective— with the positive conviction that you can, to some extent at least, take control of your life; "Go for it, " with a realistic awareness that you might not get it, but that's all right: it's the effort that matters anyway!

Mail Order Information:

    For additional copies of *Holyquest* send $8.00 per book plus $1.50 for shipping and handling (ADD 6% Sales Tax—CA Res.). Makes checks payable to Tony Perrino, 124 East Arrellaga, Santa Barbara, California 93101. Telephone (805) 962-0751.

    Also available through local bookstores that use R.R. Bowker Company BOOKS IN PRINT catalogue system. Order through through publisher SUNFLOWER INK for bookstore discount.